PRAISE FOR
Notes from No Man's Land: American Essays

* Winner of the National Book Critics Circle Award for Criticism *
* Winner of the Graywolf Press Nonfiction Prize *
* A *Time Out Chicago* Best Book of the Year *
* A *School Library Journal* Best Adult Book for High School Students *

"What do a gentrifying lakeside Chicago neighborhood, the invention of telephone poles, NAFTA, and race-based adoption have in common? In Eula Biss's book of essays, *Notes from No Man's Land*, it's the formation of America—but a vision of America antic, new and varied, and as far from a melting pot as Lake Michigan. . . . By approaching her subjects sideways, Biss avoids sounding dry or clumsily political. But she also makes an implicit point—the story of our country is not straightforward, but one of unexpected siblings and strange adoptions, a story of change, adaptation, and surprising ancestry. . . . After reading *Notes from No Man's Land*, readers will have a hard time seeing America the same way, too."—Lizzie Skurnick, from her citation for the National Book Critics Circle Award

"Biss's examination of America's complicated racial heritage offers penetrating insight. In 'Back to Buxton,' she contrasts the supposedly progressive university in Iowa City, where white and black students rarely cross paths, with the early-20th-century hamlet of Buxton, a small, Jim Crow–era town that functioned, briefly, as a desegregated utopia. . . . 'Is this Kansas?,' in particular, raises some troubling questions about the way the young are trained to view tragedies like Katrina—often through the harsh lens of racial stereotypes. Telephone poles may be on their way out, but at moments like these, Biss still encourages us to reach out and connect."—*Time Out New York*

"As Biss takes us on a tour through life in New York City; San Diego; La Salina, Mexico; and Iowa, the author is not afraid to sound foolish or to show uncertainty or weakness. She contemplates the pat-downs but never does anything about them. But such candidness isn't offered up to gain our sympathy. (In fact, it's easy to forget that *Notes from No Man's Land*, cultural critique aside, is a memoir of sorts.) Instead, it is the human companion to a piercing insight that continually surprises, astonishing us with arguments we didn't even realize our author was making. Biss is telling us the story of our country—one we never saw coming."—*The Chicago Tribune*

"Biss calls our attention to things so intrinsic in our lives they have become invisible, such as telephone poles and our assumptions about race. . . . Matters of race, sense of self, and belonging involve everyone, and Biss's crossing-the-line perspective will provoke fresh analysis of our fears and expectations."

—Donna Seaman, *Booklist* (starred review)

"Whether pointing out the self-serving hypocrisy of modern institutional agendas or rewriting Joan Didion's famous 'Goodbye to All That,' Biss's steady gaze is invaluable to the contemporary essay. . . . Reading this book will force you to take a long, hard look at what's going on in a no man's land near you."   —*Rain Taxi Review of Books*

"Expository writing should always be this compelling, provocative, and intelligent. Biss explores race in America through multiple lenses, examining common issues through uncommon situations and events. She flawlessly weaves present-day experiences with historical research to create 13 essays that combine narrative appeal with fascinating facts."   —*School Library Journal*

"With surgical-grade prose and an earnest, unrelenting pursuit of uncomfortable truths, Biss explores what it means to live in America, fitting herself into a long tradition of incisive observers from Alexis de Tocqueville to DuBois to Joan Didion."

—*The Georgia Review*

"Although plenty critical examinations of race already exist, Biss's approach to the subject is fueled by a quest for intellectual clarity so intense that it takes on a spiritual tone. These essays are also confessions, the revelations of a disappointed and sensitive thinker. She welcomes disillusionment again and again, a process both painful and transcendent."   —*Venus Zine*

"An intense, sensitive author and journalist with a restless spirit and a whip-crack wit, Biss presents a collection of short essays on race in America that spans an impressive range, beginning with a gripping narrative connecting the history of the telephone pole with the history of lynching. As her stories progress, Biss extrapolates a great deal about America's complicated racial attitudes from her own experience— teaching in Harlem, living in a diverse Chicago neighborhood, watching the long, sad saga of Hurricane Katrina from Iowa. The result is a personal, opinionated and accessible collection; Americans of any background, while they may disagree with her point of view, will see a country they recognize in settings as diverse as deepest Brooklyn or a Mexican border retreat."   —*Publishers Weekly*

"Biss writes, 'I apologize for slavery.' It's less an admission of wrongdoing than a classic apologia—a formal defense, and implicit examination, of her own conduct, which is what underpins this entire book. The reader is once again reminded of those telephone poles at the turn of the twentieth century, which served as both gallows and technological thruway. That nexus implicates all of us, and Biss puts it in plain view: for a moment, at least, we see even what is unseen."—*Columbia Journalism Review*

"Biss's pairings of ideas, like those of most original thinkers, have the knack of seeming brilliant and obvious at the same time. The book's first essay, 'Time and Distance Overcome,' intersperses brief fragments on the creation of our country's network of telephone poles with the history of another American innovation: lynching. 'Relations' weaves the story of Biss's extended mixed-race family with that of the case of the white Long Island woman mistakenly impregnated with the embryo of a black couple. And 'No Man's Land,' one of the most affecting and original essays published in this decade, uses the childhood pioneer story of *Little House on the Prairie* author Laura Ingalls Wilder to examine Biss's unreasoning fear of her new black neighbors after moving to the Rogers Park section of Chicago. . . . Without a hint of self-indulgence, Biss is repeatedly able to use her own experience to make astonishing assertions. . . . *Notes from No Man's Land* is, as Biss writes, a book about absolution. But these forceful, beautiful essays don't simply want us to move on. They want us to move forward together."—Lizzie Skurnick, National Public Radio

"I can hardly speak of this book, honestly: it's heartrendingly amazing and so completely/complexly itself that the idea of trying to encapsulate it is laughable. What it is, for sure, is this: it's Eula Biss wondering about and poring over and looping back on/ through ideas about race and self and home and America. I know that that process— someone at the wheel, driving into the big dark map of self/race/America—is only fully magnificent in the hands/words of a few artists, but let's here be totally clear that Eula Biss is one of those artists, someone whose work, if made mandatory consumption for the country, would enrich and enlarge each of us to a point of fullness that's almost scary. It's really that good a book, seriously: buy it for yourself, and then buy ten copies, hand them out to friends, start petitions to get a national Eula Biss day."
—*Corduroy Books*

"Biss's undertaking, then, is to lead us into no man's land by uncovering how we're already there. Drawing upon stories from the media, historical records, sociological research, and her own keenly observed experiences, she demonstrates how the legacy of racism has left the U.S. a kind of disputed ground, a place of confusion where whites and blacks may find belonging within their own racial groups but struggle to belong together as Americans. . . . As a white woman from a multiracial family who grew up with African traditions, Biss interrogates her own whiteness and the privileges it confers on her but finds no easy answers. . . . Yet for all her questions and uncertainty, Biss doesn't leave us in no man's land. She sees a way forward in repentance, the possibility of our collective salvation."—*The Literary Review*

"'Gangs are real, but they are also conceptual,' Eula Biss says, and the wide embrace of that observation speaks well for her essays, which are always ideologically alive even as they are grounded in fascinating details: children's dolls, the history of telephone poles, the saga of the Hanging Gardens of Babylon. But this book is no miscellany. All of Biss's explorations finally address race in the United States, from someone whose life seems devoted to that great pondering . . . and so this is an essential (and quintessential) American book."—Albert Goldbarth

"These essays are a brave and honest account of Biss's journeys through space and the inner self. Like Blake, that other mystic poet, she sees the world in a grain of sand. Without missing a beat, she looks at a telephone pole as a symbol of our universal connection, the intrusion of technology, an instrument of lynch mobs, a reminder of her grandfather's death, and a symbol of life sprouting new leaves even after it is strung with wires. Every page sparkles with imagination."—Noel Ignatiev

"Biss's occasions, whether race, identity, geography, space, heredity, or fate, are intractable, even impossible, yet her intricate command and the elegance of her mind in motion originate in doubt, distrust, and self-skepticism. Biss writes essays the way Plutarch and Montaigne did—also think James Baldwin, Anne Carson, Jenny Boully, and Luc Sante."—Robert Polito, Judge, Graywolf Press Nonfiction Prize

Notes from No Man's Land

ALSO BY EULA BISS

The Balloonists

Notes from No Man's Land

AMERICAN ESSAYS

Eula Biss

Graywolf Press

Publication of this volume is made possible in part by a grant provided by the Minnesota State Arts
Board, through an appropriation by the Minnesota State Legislature; a grant from the Wells Fargo
Foundation Minnesota; and a grant from the National Endowment for the Arts, which believes that
a great nation deserves great art. Significant support has also been provided by the Bush Foundation;
Target; the McKnight Foundation; and other generous contributions from foundations, corpora-
tions, and individuals. To these organizations and individuals we offer our heartfelt thanks.

The Graywolf Press Nonfiction Prize is funded in part by endowed
gifts from the Arsham Ohanessian Charitable Remainder Unitrust and
the Ruth Easton Fund of the Edelstein Family Foundation.

Published by Graywolf Press
250 Third Avenue North, Suite 600
Minneapolis, Minnesota 55401
All rights reserved.
www.graywolfpress.org

Published in the United States of America

ISBN 978-1-55597-518-0

10 12 14 13 11 9

Library of Congress Control Number: 2008935599

Cover design and art: Quemadura

For my baby,
who doesn't have a name yet.

Contents

Before

Time and Distance Overcome

"Of what use is such an invention?" the *New York World* asked shortly after Alexander Graham Bell first demonstrated his telephone in 1876. The world was not waiting for the telephone.

Bell's financial backers asked him not to work on his new invention because it seemed too dubious an investment. The idea on which the telephone depended—the idea that every home in the country could be connected by a vast network of wires suspended from poles set an average of one hundred feet apart—seemed far more unlikely than the idea that the human voice could be transmitted through a wire.

Even now it is an impossible idea, that we are all connected, all of us.

"At the present time we have a perfect network of gas pipes and water pipes throughout our large cities," Bell wrote to his business partners in defense of his idea. "We have main pipes laid under the streets communicating by side pipes with the various dwellings. . . . In a similar manner it is conceivable that cables of telephone wires could be laid under ground, or suspended overhead, communicating by branch wires with private dwellings, counting houses, shops, manufactories, etc., uniting them through the main cable."

Imagine the mind that could imagine this. That could see us joined by one branching cable. This was the mind of a man who wanted to invent, more than the telephone, a machine that would allow the deaf to hear.

For a short time the telephone was little more than a novelty. For twenty-five cents you could see it demonstrated by Bell himself, in a church, along with singing and recitations by local talent. From some distance away, Bell would receive a call from "the invisible Mr. Watson." Then the telephone became a plaything of the rich. A Boston banker paid for a private line between his office and his home so that he could let his family know exactly when he would be home for dinner.

Mark Twain was among the first Americans to own a telephone, but he wasn't completely taken with the device. "The human voice carries entirely too far as it is," he remarked.

By 1889, the New York Times was reporting a "War on Telephone Poles." Wherever telephone companies were erecting poles, home owners and business owners were sawing them down or defending their sidewalks with rifles.

Property owners in Red Bank, New Jersey, threatened to tar and feather the workers putting up telephone poles. A judge granted a group of home owners an injunction to prevent the telephone company from erecting any new poles. Another judge found that a man who had cut down a pole because it was "obnoxious" was not guilty of malicious mischief.

Telephone poles, newspaper editorials complained, were an urban blight. The poles carried a wire for each telephone— sometimes hundreds of wires. And in some places there were also telegraph wires, power lines, and trolley cables. The sky was netted with wires.

The war on telephone poles was fueled, in part, by that terribly American concern for private property, and a reluctance to surrender it for a shared utility. And then there was a fierce sense of aesthetics, an obsession with purity, a dislike for the way the poles and wires marred a landscape that those other new inventions, skyscrapers and barbed wire, were just beginning to complicate. And then perhaps there was also a fear that distance, as it had always been known and measured, was collapsing.

The city council in Sioux Falls, South Dakota, ordered policemen to cut down all the telephone poles in town. And the mayor of Oshkosh, Wisconsin, ordered the police chief and the fire department to chop down the telephone poles there. Only one pole was chopped down before the telephone men climbed all the poles along the line, preventing any more chopping. Soon, Bell Telephone Company began stationing a man at the top of each pole as soon as it had been set, until enough poles had been set to string a wire between them, at which point it became a misdemeanor to interfere with the poles. Even so, a constable cut down two poles holding forty or fifty wires. And a home owner sawed down a recently wired pole, then fled from police. The owner of a cannery ordered his workers to throw dirt back into the hole the telephone company was digging in front of his building. His men threw the dirt back in as fast as the telephone workers could dig it out. Then he sent out a team with a load of stones to dump into the hole. Eventually, the pole was erected on the other side of the street.

Despite the war on telephone poles, it would take only four years after Bell's first public demonstration of the telephone for every town of more than ten thousand people to be wired, although many towns were wired only to themselves. By the turn of the century, there were more telephones than bathtubs in America.

"Time and dist. overcome," read an early advertisement for the telephone. Rutherford B. Hayes pronounced the installation of a telephone in the White House "one of the greatest events since creation." The telephone, Thomas Edison declared, "annihilated time and space, and brought the human family in closer touch."

In 1898, in Lake Cormorant, Mississippi, a black man was hanged from a telephone pole. And in Weir City, Kansas. And in Brookhaven, Mississippi. And in Tulsa, Oklahoma, where the hanged man was riddled with bullets. In Danville, Illinois, a black man's throat was slit, and his dead body was strung up on a telephone pole. Two black men were hanged from a telephone pole in Lewisburg, West Virginia. And two in Hempstead, Texas, where one man was dragged out of the courtroom by a mob, and another was dragged out of jail.

A black man was hanged from a telephone pole in Belleville, Illinois, where a fire was set at the base of the pole and the man was cut down half-alive, covered in coal oil, and burned. While his body was burning the mob beat it with clubs and cut it to pieces.

Lynching, the first scholar of the subject determined, is an American invention. Lynching from bridges, from arches, from trees standing alone in fields, from trees in front of the county courthouse, from trees used as public billboards, from trees barely able to support the weight of a man, from telephone poles, from streetlamps, and from poles erected solely for that purpose. From the middle of the nineteenth century to the middle of the twentieth century, black men were lynched for crimes real and imagined, for whistles, for rumors, for "disputing with a white man," for "unpopularity," for "asking a white woman in marriage," for "peeping in a window."

The children's game of telephone depends on the fact that a message passed quietly from one ear to another to another will get distorted at some point along the line.

More than two hundred antilynching bills were introduced to the U.S. Congress during the twentieth century, but none were passed. Seven presidents lobbied for antilynching legislation, and the House of Representatives passed three separate measures, each of which was blocked by the Senate.

In Pine Bluff, Arkansas, a black man charged with kicking a white girl was hanged from a telephone pole. In Longview, Texas, a black man accused of attacking a white woman was hanged from a telephone pole. In Greenville, Mississippi, a black man accused of attacking a white telephone operator was hanged from a telephone pole. "The negro only asked time to pray." In Purcell, Oklahoma, a black man accused of attacking a white woman was tied to a telephone pole and burned. "Men and women in automobiles stood up to watch him die."

The poles, of course, were not to blame. It was only coincidence that they became convenient as gallows, because they were tall and straight, with a crossbar, and because they stood in public places. And it was only coincidence that the telephone poles so closely resembled crucifixes.

Early telephone calls were full of noise. "Such a jangle of meaningless noises had never been heard by human ears," Herbert Casson wrote in his 1910 *History of the Telephone*. "There were spluttering and bubbling, jerking and rasping, whistling and screaming."

In Shreveport, Lousiana, a black man charged with attacking a white girl was hanged from a telephone pole. "A knife was left sticking in the body." In Cumming, Georgia, a black man accused of assaulting a white girl was shot repeatedly, then hanged from a telephone pole. In Waco, Texas, a black man convicted of killing a white woman was taken from the courtroom by a mob and burned, then his charred body was hanged from a telephone pole.

A postcard was made from the photo of a burned man hanging from a telephone pole in Texas, his legs broken off below the knee and his arms curled up and blackened. Postcards of lynchings were sent out as greetings and warnings until 1908, when the postmaster general declared them unmailable. "This is the barbecue we had last night," reads one.

"If we are to die," W. E. B. DuBois wrote in 1911, "in God's name let us perish like men and not like bales of hay." And "if we must die," Claude McKay wrote ten years later, "let it not be like hogs."

In Pittsburg, Kansas, a black man was hanged from a telephone pole, cut down, burned, shot, and stoned with bricks. "At first the negro was defiant," the *New York Times* reported, "but just before he was hanged he begged hard for his life."

In the photographs, the bodies of the men lynched from telephone poles are silhouetted against the sky. Sometimes two men to a pole, hanging above the buildings of a town. Sometimes three. They hang like flags in still air.

In Cumberland, Maryland, a mob used a telephone pole as a battering ram to break into the jail where a black man charged with the murder of a policeman was being held. They kicked him to death, then fired twenty shots into his head. They wanted to burn his body, but a minister asked them not to.

The lynchings happened everywhere, in all but four states. From shortly before the invention of the telephone to long after the first transatlantic call. More in the South, and more in rural areas. In the cities and in the North, there were race riots.

Riots in Cincinnati, New Orleans, Memphis, New York, Atlanta, Philadelphia, Houston . . .

During the race riots that destroyed the black section of Springfield, Ohio, a black man was shot and hanged from a telephone pole.

During the race riots that set fire to East St. Louis and forced five hundred black people to flee their homes, a black man was hanged from a telephone pole. The rope broke and his body fell into the gutter. "Negros are lying in the gutters every few feet in some places," read the newspaper account.

In 1921, the year before Bell died, four companies of the National Guard were called out to end a race war in Tulsa that began when a white woman accused a black man of rape. Bell had lived to complete the first call from New York to San Francisco, which required 14,000 miles of copper wire and 130,000 telephone poles.

My grandfather was a lineman. He broke his back when a telephone pole fell. "Smashed him onto the road," my father says.

When I was young, I believed that the arc and swoop of telephone wires along the roadways was beautiful. I believed that the telephone poles, with their transformers catching the evening sun, were glorious. I believed my father when he said, "My dad could raise a pole by himself." And I believed that the telephone itself was a miracle.

Now, I tell my sister, these poles, these wires, do not look the same to me. Nothing is innocent, my sister reminds me. But nothing, I would like to think, remains unrepentant.

One summer, heavy rains fell in Nebraska and some green telephone poles grew small leafy branches.

New York

Relations

In New York City, in the spring of 1999, a story hit the newspapers of a Staten Island woman who had given birth to twins—one white and one black. The woman and her husband were white and the black baby was not theirs, at least not biologically. The embryo that became that baby had been accidentally implanted in the woman's uterus with the embryo of her biological son, but it belonged to a black couple who were clients at the same fertility clinic, and they wanted their son back. After a DNA test, a custody battle, a state supreme-court ruling, and an unsuccessful appeal, it was decided that the black baby was the child of the black couple, legally and entirely.

The story had its peculiarities, like the fact that the fertility clinic notified the black couple that some of their embryos had been mistakenly implanted in another woman but did not tell them anything more, so that they eventually learned of the birth of their son through a private investigator. But even odd circumstances like this took on the sheen of metaphor, pointing, for those of us who were looking, to further evidence of a systematic failure of any number of services to reach black people intact, in the form in which they are typically enjoyed by white people. If both babies had been white, I doubt the story would have become the parable it became, playing out in the newspapers over the next few years as an epic tale of blood and belonging.

The fact that the story involved two babies and two mothers and, eventually, an agreement that gave both babies a family and both families a baby, would inspire some reporters to use the phrase "happy ending," but the story would resist that happy ending for quite some time, in part because the black baby was initially returned to his biological parents on the strict condition that he would continue to visit his twin brother, spending a week in summer and alternate holidays with the white family. On the question of whether a person can have a twin to whom he is not related, the New Jersey *Record* consulted an expert, who explained that the babies were not technically twins but that their situation was so unusual it was impossible to determine, without further research, how deep a bond they might share. Long after the black baby had been returned to his biological parents and given a new name, the question of what exactly his relationship was to the white baby persisted. The answer to this question would determine whether or not the courts would mandate visits between the black boy and the white family. "Are the baby boys brothers in the eyes of the law," asked the *New York Times*, "or two separate people who just happened to arrive in the world on the same subway car?"

When we were young, my sister and I had two baby dolls that were exactly alike in every way except that one was white and one was black. The precise sameness of these dolls, so obviously cast from one mold in two different colors of plastic, convinced me that they were, like us, sisters.

There is no biological basis for what we call race, meaning that most human variation occurs within individual "races" rather than between them. Race is a social fiction. But it is also, for now at least, a social fact. We may be remarkably genetically similar, but we are not all, culturally speaking, the same. And if that Long Island woman had raised the black boy to whom she gave birth, he might have been robbed of a certain amount of the cultural identity to which his skin would be assigned later in life and might therefore find himself, as an adult, in an uncomfortable no man's land between two racial identities.

But this no man's land is already fairly heavily trafficked. Without denying that blacks and whites remain largely segregated and disturbingly polarized, and without denying that black culture is a distinct, if not uniform, culture, I think we ought to admit, as the writer Albert Murray once insisted, that American culture is "incontestably mulatto." A friend of mine used to tell a story about a segregated restaurant in the South where a sign on one side of the room advertised "Home Cooking" and a sign on the other advertised "Soul Food" and the customers on both sides were eating the same biscuits and gravy. "For all their traditional antagonisms and obvious differences," Murray wrote in *The Omni-Americans,* "the so-called black and so-called white people of the United States resemble nobody else in the world so much as they resemble each other."

Even so, we don't tend to make family out of one another. Marriages between whites and blacks amount to fewer than 1 percent of all our marriages. And even after the last state laws banning interracial marriage were declared unconstitutional in 1967, some states continued to ban interracial adoptions. The agencies that first began placing black children with white couples often viewed these placements as highly progressive. Not everyone agreed. The National Association of Black Social Workers, in particular, has continued to oppose the adoption of black children by white parents ever since the release of their somewhat notorious 1972 statement on the preservation of black families, which suggested that the likely outcome of such adoptions was "cultural genocide."

The bitterness of this statement, and its refusal to see white Americans as viable parents for black Americans, is probably best understood in the context of all the wrong that has been done to black children by white adults in this country. There was, during slavery, the use of black women for "breeding" purposes, the forced infidelities of that system, the denial of slave marriages as legitimate contracts, and the practice of selling members of the same family away from each other, so that sisters were separated from brothers, mothers were separated from fathers, and young children were separated from one or both parents. More than a century after emancipation, we still have the unmanning of black men by law enforcement, the incommensurate imprisonment of black fathers, and the troubling biases of the child-welfare system, in which a disproportionate number of black children are separated from their parents.

That doesn't mean white adults can't be good parents for black children, but the endeavor is fraught with history and complicated by all our current social failures. If the white woman on Staten Island had given birth to two white babies, it might have been easier to ignore one of the uglier elements of her story: the fact that our claim on our children amounts to a kind of ownership. At one point, the biological parents of the black baby decided that they would rather pay the $200,000 fine mandated by their shared-custody agreement than continue to allow the white couple visits with their son. The white couple balked at this, and their lawyer said, "They're not looking to, quote, 'sell' their son!"

If both babies had been white, I might have felt that the white woman was entitled to keep them both, no matter whom they were related to. I might have been wrong, and the courts would very probably not have agreed with me, but I would have believed in her right to keep any child she carried in her womb because that is what I would want for myself. As it was, because one of those babies was black, and because the black woman did not herself conceive—her treatments at the fertility clinic failed and she was childless—it did not seem right for the white woman to keep the black baby. It seemed like a kind of robbery, a robbery made worse by its echoes of history. But even still—and perhaps this exposes exactly how wishful I really am—I wanted to believe in the white woman's desire to maintain a familial connection with the black child. I wanted the two boys to be brothers, and I wanted the original shared-custody agreement to work out. And it might have, especially if the white woman had not made the mistake of saying "come to Mommy" to the black baby on one of those visits, and of calling him by the name she had given him, which was no longer his name.

The white doll was my sister's and the black doll was mine. My doll's proper name was Susannah, but her common name, the name I used more often, and the name my entire family used, was Black Doll. My mother finds this hilarious, but I don't enjoy revealing it. Even so, when I was young the fact that Black Doll was black became very ordinary to me very quickly, so that her name was nothing but her name.

The famous "doll studies" of Mamie and Kenneth Clark, which were conducted in a series of different schools in both the North and the South starting in 1939, used a set of identical black and white baby dolls bought at a Woolworth's in Harlem to reveal how racism affected children. In one experiment, sixteen black children were shown a white doll and a black doll and asked to pick which doll best represented certain words. Eleven of the children associated the black doll with the word "bad" and ten associated the white doll with the word "nice." This experiment later influenced the *Brown v. Board of Education* decision to integrate the public schools.

In the years and decades following that decision, questions would be raised about what exactly, if anything, the doll studies proved. Black children in unsegregated schools had responded to the Clarks' dolls in much the same way as black children in segregated schools, which complicated the idea that the children were responding solely to segregation. But they were clearly responding to something. Perhaps the doll studies suggest that children are as sensitive to racial codes as adults. I do not know exactly how the word "nice" was used in 1939 but I do know what it means now to describe a neighborhood as "nice" or another part of town as "bad" and I know what "nice" hair is and I know what it means when my landlady tells me, as I'm applying for a lease, that she won't need my bank account number because I look like a "nice" person. And

I suspect it is possible, especially in a racially aware environment, that the secondary meanings of these words are not lost even on six-year-olds.

"Maybe we love our dolls because we can't love ourselves," a friend of mine—an artist who made drawings of dolls missing legs or arms or eyes, that all looked, somehow, eerily like her—once suggested. Perhaps this is the essential truth behind why we make effigies. And maybe this is why we tend to believe that children should have dolls that look like them, or at least that look like what they might eventually become. In 1959, Mattel introduced a doll that was, unlike most other dolls marketed for children, not a baby doll. This doll had breasts and wore makeup and was modeled after a doll sold in Germany as a gag gift for grown men. The man who designed the American version of the doll, a man who had formerly designed Sparrow and Hawk missiles for the Pentagon and was briefly married to Zsa Zsa Gabor, was charged with making the new Barbie doll look less like a "German street walker," which he attempted in part by filing off her nipples.

In the past few decades, quite a few people have suggested—citing most often the offense of impossible proportions—that Barbie dolls teach young girls to hate themselves. But the opposite may be true. British researchers recently found that girls between the ages of seven and eleven harbor surprisingly strong feelings of dislike for their Barbie dolls, with no other toy or brand name inspiring such a negative response from the children. The dolls "provoked rejection, hatred, and violence," and many girls preferred Barbie torture—by cutting, burning, decapitating, or microwaving—over other ways of playing with the doll. Reasons that the girls hated their Barbies included, somewhat poetically, the fact that they were "plastic." The researchers also noted that the girls never spoke of one single, special Barbie, but tended to talk about having a box full of anonymous Barbies. "On a deeper level Barbie has become inanimate," one of the researchers remarked. "She has lost any individual warmth that she might have possessed if she were perceived as a singular person. This may go some way towards explaining the violence and torture."

My own Black Doll, who is now kept by my mother as a memento of my childhood, was loved until the black of her hair and the pink of her lips rubbed off. Her skin is pocked with marks where I pricked her with needles, administering immunizations. She wears a dress that my grandmother sewed for her. And she has, stored in a closet somewhere, a set of furniture made for her by the German cabinetmaker who boarded with my family when I was young. There is something moving to me now about the idea of that man, who left Germany in the 1920s, just as the Nazi party was gathering power, laboring at his lathe, perfecting the fancy legs of a maple dining table for a beloved toy known as Black Doll.

Although the two can be confused, our urge to love our own, or those we have come to understand as our own, is, it seems, much more powerful than our urge to segregate ourselves. And perhaps this is why that Staten Island woman went to court to fight for shared custody of a child who was very clearly, very publicly, no blood relation to her or her husband. It was an act of thievery, but it was also an act of love.

In the agonized handwritten statement she released to the press just before she voluntarily surrendered to his biological parents the four-month-old child to whom she gave birth, long before the court decision that would decide she had no right to share custody of him, the white woman said, "We're giving him up because we love him." She had come to believe that it was in the best interest of the black baby to be with his biological parents. In a separate statement, her lawyer added, "She didn't look at them as a white baby and a black baby. She looked at them as her sons." This was already quite evident from the fact that she had insisted on a DNA test before she would consider giving the child back to the black couple whose embryos—as she had been informed by the fertility clinic—were implanted in her womb.

A group of white children and a group of black children were asked, in one of the Clarks' doll studies, to choose the baby doll that looked the most like them. The white children overwhelmingly chose the white doll. But seven of the sixteen black children also chose the white doll. Some of the others could not choose a doll, and a few broke into tears.

As a teenager I sometimes posed for my mother's sculptures. She worked in black porcelain, which is, when fired, as deep and rich a black as white porcelain is a cool and flawless white. At that time, my mother had just converted to a West African religion and was dating a black man. Her friends were black women and Puerto Rican women, and her imagination was full of African folklore. I posed for a mask she was making of the face of Oya—Yoruba goddess of the graveyard, of wind, and of change—standing in her attic studio with my lips pursed as though I were blowing. Why should I have been surprised, and somewhat hurt, when the mask was finished, to see that my face had become unmistakably African? My eyes were still almond-shaped, as they are, but my cheekbones were higher, my nose was flatter and wider, and my lips were fuller. Still, my face was in that face—I could see it there, especially in the mouth.

The topsy-turvy doll is a traditional doll peculiar to the United States. These dolls have heads on both ends of their bodies and wear skirts that can be flipped up or down to reveal either one head or the other. In the antebellum South, many of these dolls had a white head on one end and a black head on the other. Some topsy-turvy dolls were sold with the slogan "Turn me up and turn me back, first I'm white, and then I'm black."

The possibility of moving, through disguise, between one race and another is an idea so compelling that it keeps returning to us, again and again. There was Nella Larsen's *Passing,* John Howard Griffin's *Black Like Me,* Eddie Murphy's *Saturday Night Live* skit in which he dressed as a white man and discovered that banks give money away to white people, and, most recently, there was *Black. White.,* a reality television show produced by R. J. Cutler and Ice Cube, an experiment that put two families, one white and one black, in a house together and used Hollywood makeup to switch their races.

I have a cousin whose race is sometimes perceived as black and other times as white. Her father is a black man from Jamaica, and her mother is my mother's sister. My cousin and I grew up on opposite sides of the country, she in Oakland, California, and I in upstate New York, but we both found ourselves in New York City in our twenties, and we shared an apartment in Brooklyn for a year. When I moved to New York I barely knew my cousin, but I was comforted by the idea that she was family. My cousin and I come from an extended family in which it is generally understood that even the most remote members cannot be strangers to each other.

And we were not. We looked alike, but in an oblique way that was probably most striking to us, because my cousin looked very much like my mother, and I looked very much like hers, but neither of us looked like our own mother. Beyond that, we recognized in each other the distinctively frugal and, we decided, hereditary habit of washing and saving bits of tinfoil and plastic sandwich bags. Neither of us seemed, by nature, capable of working full-time, and we were always saving our money so that we could afford not to work. We both slept very poorly in the city, and we both considered ourselves in exile there. Both of us were inexplicably moved by the concrete cross outside our living room window. And we both had the same characteristic gesture of putting one of our hands to our neck protectively. We reveled in this sameness, in this twinning. We even called each other by the same name. "Cousin!" I would sing as I walked in the door. "Is that you, Cousin?" she would answer.

At some point during the year we lived together, I watched my cousin cut out pictures of black college beauty queens from *Ebony* magazine and glue them into a notebook. She didn't know what she wanted to do with them yet, she told me, she'd have to think about it. But she lined them up lovingly—Miss Norfolk State University, Miss Morris College, Miss Florida A&M University, Miss North Carolina Agricultural and Technical State University, Miss Southern University—like a paper-doll parade replete with heartbreaking plastic crowns and tiaras.

Years later, my cousin would send me a film called *A Girl Like Me,* in which a seventeen-year-old girl from New York re-creates the Clarks' doll studies at a Harlem day-care center. In this 2005 re-creation, fifteen of twenty-one black children prefer the white doll over the black doll. "Can you show me the doll that looks bad?" a voice behind the camera asks a little black girl. The child immediately chooses the black doll, and when she is asked why, she reports flatly, "Because she's black." But when the voice asks her, "Can you give me the doll that looks like you?" she looks down, first reaching for the white doll but then, looking directly at the camera, reluctantly pushing the black doll forward.

As Barbie dolls became increasingly popular in the sixties, Barbie's family expanded to include her boyfriend Ken, her little sister Skipper, her twin siblings Tutti and Todd, and her cousin Francie. In 1967, Mattel released Colored Francie, a black version of Cousin Francie. Notably, Colored Francie was intended to be understood as a friend for Barbie, not a cousin. One of the many objections to Colored Francie was that she was cast out of the same mold as the white Francie and therefore had the same face and the same features. This oversight was seen by some as hostile, as another attempt to erase the Africanness of

African Americans. Colored Francie did not sell well, and she was soon discontinued.

Despite this early failure, Mattel has maintained a long-standing tradition of releasing both a black version and a white version of many of their dolls. This was most problematic in 1997, when they teamed up with Nabisco to promote Oreo Fun Barbie. The cheerfulness of the black Oreo Fun Barbie, who was sold in packaging covered with pictures of Oreo cookies and whose dress was emblazoned with the word "Oreo," seemed to mock, chillingly, the predicament of the *Oreo*—the person who is seen as black on the outside but white on the inside. Oreo Fun Barbie was quickly recalled when Mattel realized that she evoked cultural abdication and self-loathing.

As a child, my cousin worried that her mother loved her brother more because he was not as brown as she was. Even so, her skin is light enough to "pass." That was a household word for us in those days when we lived together. I remember, in particular, an evening when I invited a graduate student I'd met at a party over for dinner. We listened to Neil Young and talked about World War II, and sized each other up as material for love. When he left, just after I closed the door behind him, my cousin shot me a look. "What?" I said. "You were passing," she said, meaning that I had not been acting like myself. And she was right, although at the time I resented her accuracy.

Someone once accused my mother of adopting the identity of whichever man she was with. It does seem that my mother has been trying to escape her own white, Protestant, middle-class background ever since she dropped out of high school and got on a Greyhound bus, but shouldn't she be allowed out if she wants out? Especially now that she has sacrificed, in various ways, just about all the privilege to which she could ever have laid claim. A multiracial society, Randall Kennedy recently wrote, "ought to allow its members free entry into and exit from racial categories."

If they are willing to make any sort of nod toward the existence of race as a legitimate category, most scientists agree that a person's race is self-identified, and the U.S. census now categorizes people only as they self-identify. But our racial categories are so closely policed by the culture at large that it would be much more accurate to say that we are collectively identified. Whenever we range outside the racial identity that has been collectively assigned to us, we are very quickly reminded where we belong.

Not long after I moved into my cousin's apartment in the historically black neighborhood of Fort Greene, I stopped at a small shop a few blocks away to buy her a birthday present of some hair oil I'd seen her admire. I was standing with my back to the register choosing between Nubian Woman and Jasmine, when I heard loud whispers and laughter from behind me. "White girl!" the saleswomen were saying, with every intention I would hear them.

In that part of Brooklyn, the people I passed on the street often greeted me with a summary description of what they noticed about me, as in, "You've got some short hair, girl." This was a phenomenon that my cousin and I found both arresting and amusing. For her part, my cousin discovered that the indicators of race she had learned in Oakland did not necessarily translate to Brooklyn. The way she walked, for example, the sharp switch of her gait, might have been read as black in Oakland, but it was not in Brooklyn. Here her identity became even more ambiguous. Walking home through the park after dark one night, my cousin passed a black man who nodded at her and said, "Mmm-hmmm, you're a bad-ass white girl."

I was mistaken for a white boy twice, and once I was mistaken for Asian. But I was never taken for black. And I could not have expected to be. As much as I believe racial categories to be fluid and ambiguous, I still know that there is nothing particularly ambiguous about my features, or my bearing, or my way of speaking. And although I was familiar, from my mother's religion, with the cowry shells and oiled wood carvings sold in the African shops of my neighborhood, I could not pass there.

At the beginning of the six-episode series *Black. White.*, the white family needs coaching from the black family in order to learn how to pass as black. But the black family, as they explain after an uncomfortable silence, already knows how to act white, of course, because that is the dominant culture within which they have to live their daily lives. Knowing how to act white is a survival skill for the black family. The white family, on the other hand, struggles with acting black, frequently committing tone-deaf errors and ultimately not quite pulling it off.

Perhaps my inability to pass is part of why I feel so trapped within my identity as a white woman. That identity does not feel chosen by me as much as it feels grudgingly defaulted to. But I haven't worked to assimilate into any other racial group. And I have rarely turned down any of the privileges my skin has afforded me. When it became clear to me, for instance, that my landlady was looking for a "nice" tenant, I did not inform her that if she was under the impression I was white, she should at least know I was not nice.

In my mostly white high school, where the white boys who listened to rap and sagged their pants were called "wiggers," we were trained to feel disdain for anyone who ranged outside the cultural confines of whiteness. But later, in my mostly white college, among wiggers and punks and hippies and tattooed freaks, I began to understand the significance of the effort to advertise one's resistance to the mainstream and undo one's access to privilege through a modification of one's clothing or body or skin. Even so, my college was such a safe and nurturing place for misfits, especially rich misfits, that it was hard to believe dreadlocks and tattoos and piercings would really inhibit anyone's ability to get a job—they certainly weren't getting in the way of anyone's ability to get an education. And many of the punks and hippies whom I went to school with have now, after all that effort, found their way into positions of power and privilege.

But I still believe it is important for white folks to find ways to signal that we cannot necessarily be trusted to act like white folks—that we cannot be trusted to hold white values, that we cannot be trusted to be nice, that we cannot be trusted to maintain the status quo. Noel Ignatiev, editor of the journal *Race Traitor,* has suggested that the power of the entire white race can be undermined by just a few members who consistently refuse to act according to the rules and who refuse to be who they seem to be. At the end of the *Saturday Night Live* skit in which he was made up as a white man, Eddie Murphy suggested exactly this possibility. "I got a lot of friends, and we've got a lot of makeup," he told the camera. "So the next time you're hugging up with some really super groovy white guy, or you've met a really great super keen white chick, don't be too sure. They might be black."

What exactly it means to be white seems to elude no one as fully as it eludes those of us who are white. In *Playing in the Dark: Whiteness and the Literary Imagination*, Toni Morrison observes that the literature of this country is full of images of impenetrable, inarticulate whiteness. And these images, she writes, are often set against the presence of black characters who are dead or powerless. She cites, as one example, Edgar Allan Poe's *The Narrative of Arthur Gordon Pym*, which ends with the death of a black man in a boat that is traveling on a milky white sea through a white shower toward a white veil behind which a giant white figure waits silently.

And so it is not surprising that what Marlow, the ferryboat captain in *Heart of Darkness*, finds deep in Africa, traveling on a boat manned by starving natives, is not darkness but a blinding white fog so thick it stops the boat, a white fog from behind which he hears chilling cries of grief. "Whiteness, alone, is mute, meaningless, unfathomable, pointless, frozen, veiled, curtained, dreaded, senseless, implacable. Or so our writers seem to say," writes Toni Morrison. We do not know ourselves, and, worse, we seem only occasionally to know that we do not know ourselves. "It was the whiteness of the whale that above all things appalled me," Melville tells us in *Moby-Dick*. "But how can I hope to explain myself here; and yet, in some dim, random way, explain myself I must."

"It's hard for me," my cousin mused once as we waited for a train. "I have a lot of white family." At the time, I couldn't fully appreciate what she was saying because I was hurt by the implication that I was a burden to her. But I would remember that comment years later, when I was watching a public-television program in which Henry Louis Gates Jr. was working with genealogists to trace the family trees of a series of African Americans, including Oprah Winfrey, Quincy Jones, Whoopi Goldberg, and himself. Many of their ancestors were slaves, but the genealogists also revealed that some of their ancestors included free blacks and, of course, whites. In a particularly awkward moment, a genealogist informed Gates that one of his ancestors was a white man who fought in the Revolutionary War against Native Americans and left a will that freed his slaves. As I watched Gates struggle with that information, I saw how much the stories of our ancestors mark our identities.

It isn't easy to accept a slaveholder and an Indian killer as a grandfather, and it isn't easy to accept the legacy of whiteness as an identity. It is an identity that carries the burden of history without fostering a true understanding of the painfulness and the costs of complicity. That's why so many of us try to pretend that to be white is merely to be raceless. Perhaps it would be more productive for us to establish some collective understanding that we are all—white and black—damaged, reduced, and morally undermined by increasingly subtle systems of racial oppression and racial privilege. Or perhaps it would be better if we simply refused to be white. But I don't know what that means, really.

"I feel like an unknown quantity," my cousin remarked at some point during the year that we lived together. She was referring to the algebraic term, the unknown quantity x, which must be solved for, or defined, by the numbers in the equation around it. I remember, when I first encountered algebra, feeling the limits of my own comprehension break around the concept that one number in an equation could be unknown. And what baffled me most was that the answer, in algebra, was known, but the question was incomplete.

I could see two faces of the Brooklyn clock tower from my bedroom window in the apartment I shared with my cousin. The hands on those faces never told exactly the same time, and I often chose to believe the one I most wanted to believe. I was usually late, either way. The year we lived in that apartment was the year of the 2000 census. By chance, my cousin and I were chosen to complete the long form of the census, and we were visited in person by a census taker who was charged with ensuring that this form was completed accurately.

The census taker asked us to report the highest degree or level of school we had completed, how well we spoke English, and whether we did any work for pay. For every question he asked, my cousin asked one back. It became a kind of exchange, which is how we learned that our census taker was an artist when he wasn't taking the census. I laughed when my cousin asked him why he needed to know the address where she worked, and she cut her eyes at me. "It's not for him," I said, trying to help, "it's for the government." She pursed her lips. "I come from people," she informed me, "who have learned not to trust the government."

And then there was question six: "What is this person's race?" The census taker marked the box in front of "White" for me, with no discussion, but my cousin spent quite a bit of time on this question. "What are my options?" she asked first. The list was surprisingly long for a document conceived by the government of a country that does not readily embrace subtlety or accuracy in just about any form: "White," "Black, African American, or Negro," "American Indian or Alaska Native," "Asian Indian," "Chinese," "Filipino," "Japanese," "Korean," "Vietnamese," "Other Asian," "Native Hawaiian," "Guamanian or Chamorro," "Samoan," "Other Pacific Islander," or "Some Other Race." Our census taker would list all of these options several times, stumbling over the words, until he eventually handed the form to my cousin in frustration. Part of the problem was that the list did not include her first choice—"Mixed Race." But it did, unlike the 1990 census, allow the census taker to mark more than one race. Eventually, he marked both "White" and "Black."

"He has two mothers," the Staten Island woman said of the black baby to whom she gave birth, in a brazen refusal of the very terms in which her story was being told. She abandoned this idea only after it was suggested to her that this might be confusing for the child and perhaps even damaging. But she did not abandon her belief that the two boys who shared her womb should grow up knowing each other as brothers. "She wants him to know that she carried him and that she loved him and in the end made the ultimate sacrifice," her lawyer said shortly after she surrendered the black baby to his parents. "And, secondly, she wants him to know he has a brother."

In the same statement, the white woman's lawyer also said, "The most important thing to her is that she wants this boy to know when he grows up that she didn't abandon him because of his race." If that was the most important thing to her and not simply her lawyer's bad idea of what needed to be said, then her story was even sadder than it first appeared. She already feared, when he was four months old, that the baby she birthed and held and fed would grow up to believe she was racist. She was giving him up because he was not hers, but the fact that he was not hers was all caught up, for her and for many others, in his race and her own.

It was not hard, in the end, to understand why the baby's biological parents in New Jersey were so adamantly opposed to sharing custody with this woman. And so it was all the more surprising, all the more touching, when, after the white woman had refused them contact with the baby for the first three months of his life, and after several years of custody disputes and court cases and appeals, the black couple told reporters that they still remained open to having some relationship with the white couple in the future. They suggested that when their son was "mature enough to understand his unique beginnings," they might be able to reach out to the white couple "in friendship and fellowship." They might be something less than family to each other, the black couple seemed to be suggesting, but they were more than strangers.

Three Songs of Salvage

1

At the top of the escalator at the Fifty-first Street station, a woman with a Caribbean accent shouts, "Ye must be born again." She seems to always be there, and a crowd of people seems to always be bottlenecked at the escalator. She shouts, "Ye must be born again. Ye ought to be born again. Ye have got to be born again."

The stairs next to the escalator are littered with the pamphlet she hands out, titled "Does God Love You?" I keep this pamphlet in the manila folder where I save all the pamphlets I have been handed on the street: "Suffering Soon to End!" and "Are You Ready?" and "Never Lonely" and "How to be Saved and Know It." Some command, some question, some threaten, some promise, some simply inform. I am most drawn to one that insists, "There is nothing you can do to save yourself."

When my mother's house caught fire her husband wasn't home. After finding the basement full of smoke, she saved herself and her stepdaughter. The firefighters arrived too late to save the house, but they saved my mother's little dog and her computer, on which she had been writing the story of her life.

My mother's great-great-grandfather wrote a short sketch of his life a few years before he died. The sketch records his marriages, the deaths of his family members, and the baptisms of his children. The place and date of the deaths of each of his four wives are followed by the place and date of his next marriage. "The second year 1881 was still more sad for me—my good wife departed this life just one week after my dear mother died—both in Toledo—this nearly killed me—it seems I can never get over it. In the year 1881 I married again, in the month of Sept. to Miss Lydia Seachrist of Girard, Ohio Trumbull County."

My mother was thirty-four when she left her husband, who was the father of her four children. She moved into a duplex with a poet and was initiated into the Yoruba tradition, a West African religion. A few years later, she left the poet and moved to a farmhouse with an African drummer from the Bronx.

Her great-great-grandfather preached on a traveling circuit and moved every one or two years for the entire forty-five years he served as a minister. One year on Mahoning Circuit, two years at Independence Station, then Summit Circuit, Columbiana Circuit, Warren Station, Allegheny District, Somerset District, Franklin District, Ottawa Circuit . . . One of his houses caught fire, two of his children died, and he lost his wives to brain fever, malarial fever, scarlet fever, and consumption. "God in his goodness," he wrote, "gave me the strength to carry on."

Standing in a crowded train headed uptown, which is leaving from the downtown platform, I listen to a bum scream,

"America, do you know where you're going?" A woman who will eventually deliver a speech about being born again begins to sing an aria. "Remember," a pamphlet reminds me, "God knows us better than we know ourselves." I have no doubt this is true.

My great-great-great-grandfather wrote two sketches of his life in the same notebook. The first is essentially a list of important names and events. It is twenty pages long. The second sketch appears to be an attempt to tell the story of his life in greater detail. It is twenty-five pages long. There are only a few references to how he felt. "In the month of July 1866 my wife died of consumption. I had much care—for six weeks I did not take off my clothes." The second sketch records all the same names and dates as the first, in much the same manner. It seems he couldn't tell his life any other way. The facts alone weren't enough to express what he had lived, but he didn't have anything else.

What did my great-great-great-grandfather try, and fail, to say about his life? In a moment of unusual detail, he listed the hardships and joys of the ministry as he told them to his second wife before they were married. "I told her all the unpleasant things about the Ministry—such as moving every two or three years—of living among strangers and being alone quite often—but I told her also of the good things about the Ministry—such as saving souls."

"Your soul," one of my pamphlets declares, "is worth more than all the world." Late in the evening, when I return to Sunset Park, I pass an old man who nods and says, "God bless you, sweetheart." When I put my half gallon of milk on the counter in the bodega, the man who takes my money says, "God bless you, beautiful." Waiting for the train, I sit down next to a young man who turns to me and says quietly, "God bless you."

2

It is the middle of the day in Harlem. I haven't spoken yet. As I do every other day, I walk up and down the streets, sometimes lost, carrying a clipboard and a list of addresses. I notice a red velvet curtain blowing out of a window. I am sweating. The branches of a tree grow up through the rotted roof of a building. At the top of the hill an old woman is sitting on a bench. She smiles and hands me a pamphlet titled "Are You Lonely?"

The idea that we need to be saved, and that we cannot save ourselves, strikes me as so profound as to be obvious.

"Enthusiasm," in its religious sense, implies intense devotion. It is from the Greek for "possessed by a god," and a certain fear of possession, of losing oneself, is still embedded in the word. My mother, in her enthusiasm, could not for some time speak a sentence that did not include a reference to the Yoruba tradition, her adopted religion. She made clay statues of the orishas, and stone pots for their ceremonies, and ritual masks. More than ten years after her initiation, those masks were still hanging on the walls of her house when it burned. In her kitchen, where the tiles on the ceiling melted and dripped down into the room like wax icicles, there was a mask of Obatala. His face was covered with broken glass. Obatala, in the Yoruba tradition, is the father of both insanity and wisdom. And he is, to use the language of another religion, my mother's patron saint.

Years ago I found a book of translated songs in my mother's

house. These are songs I may have once sung, but I do not know for sure, because I do not recognize the words. Still, they speak to me. The leader sings, "Mother, don't be angry," and the chorus answers, "We always greet hunger with a basket." The words are naked without their drums, and in English they have a strange taste, like the meat of lamb. The drum sings: *"Ori mì kò gbe, àyàà mi kò gbe."* Meaning: "My mind can't grasp it, neither can my soul."

My mother took us to the *bembés* where the orishas were called down. We watched the drummers sweat and the dancers shake, and we ate salty beans and rice with the other kids. We listened to the dancers sing and we sang, when we sang, in a language we did not understand. The more distance my mother put between herself and what she knew, between her mind and the words it understood, the closer she felt to the imponderable.

The smell of cigar smoke came up through the floorboards every night in those days. I closed the red metal grate in the floor, but the smell at night was not as bad as in the afternoons, which stank of goat skin stretched on the barn to dry. I fell asleep to the distant sound of drums, which I was not always entirely sure was the distant sound of drums. Rain, blood in the body, explosions in the quarry, and frogs are all drums.

There were weekends when I stood next to my dancing mother in a small, sweaty room that smelled of coconut oil and pulsed with the *batá* drums of Yoruba ritual. Everyone was dressed in white. *"Babalu Aye, Babalu Aye,"* we sang. That much I remember. "All people sleep and never awake," we might have meant to pray. *"Babalu,* please wake me up in my room."

My mother spoke often of ancestors, and I gave offerings

to mine. The purpose of this, as I understood it, was not to be saved as much as it was to save.

3

I have not lived at home for many years now, and my mother's house is gone. Those days of drumbeats and brush fires and the blood of chickens have sunk like a ship. I wonder what I have saved, other than myself?

On the street, as I reach for a pamphlet, the man who hands it to me says, "Excuse me, ma'am"—his hand is still holding one end of the pamphlet, and I am holding the other—"are you a Christian?" His eyes are eager. "No," I say quietly, pulling the pamphlet out of his hand as I begin to walk away. "Then what are you?" he shouts after me.

There were things in my mother's house that were not lost, but nonetheless could not be saved. Food sealed in tins at the back of the kitchen cabinets had the taste of burn, and pillows high in a closet had the smell of it. My mother's husband kept these things for as long as she would let him. Among the many items that were destroyed were the four old VCRs he had salvaged from other people's trash piles to fix. I sent my mother, after the fire, a box of clothes that held the smell of other houses and the shape of other bodies.

In college, I remember, the African-dance class humiliated me. Beginning dance students could perform the ritual dances of my childhood better than I could. Everything I had once thought was mine, I was learning, was borrowed or stolen or already lost to me.

But I sang the songs, as a girl, I made the offerings, and during the *bembés* I walked out across the fields with the other girls, my friends, who recommended that I rub my skin with cocoa butter. At home my mother spoke of the orishas fondly, familiarly, as if they were acquaintances of hers from long ago who had left a great impression on her in her youth.

Now, an elderly man leaning on an iron railing in Bed-Stuy advises me, "Keep your eyes on the world, okay? You pay attention to what's going on. Go home and write it all down, every single detail." This man is building a glass mosaic in his garden, surrounded by shattered sidewalks and dog shit. He stares at me intently. "But don't forget that what you have to capture is the unseen, the imponderable." He gestures into space, toward the building where the stubborn woman he loves lives. She is bent over with lupus and swollen with arthritis, but she insists on pushing her cart, painfully, to the store for cat food.

"If by years of patient suffering," reads one of my pamphlets, "God can manage to take the harshness out of my voice, then the time has been well-spent."

I never saw the wreckage of my mother's house. By the time I returned home, it had been torn down and the foundation had been dug out, and all that remained was a hole in the ground, a hole that was, as my mother observed, surprisingly small. Looking into the hole that had been a house whose old wood and glass and peeling paint I had loved, I didn't feel stricken, or lost, or orphaned, as I thought I might. I felt—and this is hard to admit—born again.

In the days and weeks after the fire, my mother's neighbors

came and helped her carry what could be saved out of the cracked shell of her house into the snow. There was an iron frying pan and some photographs with blackened glass, and there was also a candle—which had somehow survived the heat that destroyed the floors and the walls—in the shape of Buddha.

I know now that I left home and I left the drums but I didn't leave home and I didn't leave the drums. Sewer plates, jackhammers, subway trains, cars on the bridge, and basketballs are all drums.

"Two hundred hoes and two hundred cutlasses are scraping the mountain of stone," read the words of a song I might have sung in another language, in another life. "The mountain was sufficient to conquer all of them." I can't dance. I can't keep a beat. I crumple under the music. "The earth can arrange you in little heaps." Now, on a bar stool in Harlem, my blood fights against my skin to rush out and meet the sound of the congas. I want to get up and say I know this sound. It is mine. We have spent days and nights together and this sound has been inside my body. I sit silently and stare at the *conguero.*

I never learned any of the stories my mother told about the orishas. I can't spell their names. I don't remember their songs. But when I see a car in Brooklyn with the license plate ASHE, I feel a rush of recognition. It's a word I can't translate, but I know what it means. My mother is married again now, and she doesn't go to the *bembés* anymore. But I am still my mother's daughter, after all the distances I've traveled, and I believe ye must be born again. And again.

Land Mines

As adults, I think we can admit we do not always love children. We do not love their crying. We do not love boys on bikes waving sticks. We do not love the groups of teenagers that block the sidewalks. Sometimes we are afraid of them, and sometimes we hate how vulnerable they are.

The end of slavery was an important time in the development of this nation's school system. Northerners set up one of the first widespread networks of free schools in the South. This system was designed specifically for the education of freed slaves, and established public education in America as the method we use to manage large populations of our own people who frighten us.

While it was debated whether or not to allow the freed slaves to vote, and whether or not to send them back to Africa, it was already decided that they should be educated. Millions of donors, thousands of teachers, and hundreds of private aid societies poured their resources into that purpose. "Why schools?" the historian Ronald Butchart asks of this effort. "Why *only* schools?"

As a young teacher, I wanted to think that I recognized the stories of knives hidden in backpacks and batteries hurled at teachers for what they were—fearful exaggerations of the power of children—but I quickly learned that even small children in large enough numbers could knock me to the ground and keep me there. This would have been more frightening, of course, if I hadn't been brought down by a group of happily excited third graders who were trying to hug me.

I began talking about myself in the third person on my second day of teaching. I knew that this was correct, just as I knew, without anyone ever telling me, that I should not touch my students. The teachers I worked with didn't say much about being scared of children. Dialogue between us often seemed limited to bottles of antibacterial soap in the staff bathroom with notes taped to them reading, "For everyone, please use!" But now, when I tell people I used to teach in New York City public schools, they sometimes ask, "Were you afraid?"

After emancipation, many Northerners were afraid the freed slaves would come north for education. White liberals responded to this "freedmen problem" by funding, building, and staffing freedmen's schools in the South. Freed slaves were described by both Northerners and Southerners as being "like children." Like children, freed slaves in the South were socially and politically powerless. And like those freed slaves, children in the public schools of Northern cities now are dark-skinned.

Emancipation was followed by Reconstruction, and Reconstruction was followed by Redemption, the period in which "Redeemers" took control of the South. During Redemption, hundreds of black politicians were expelled from public office (there were more black senators in the 1870s than there are today), and the Fourteenth and Fifteenth amendments were undone. It wasn't until the Voting Rights Act of 1965 that the work of Reconstruction was taken up again by the government. And this Second Reconstruction was quickly followed by a Second Redemption, a reactionary period of denial and abandonment, the period, some would argue, in which we are still living.

In my first year of teaching, my students told me about another teacher who had quit suddenly. "He was gay and he got mad!" The story came out slowly as I asked more questions. A kid had yelled "faggot" at the teacher one day. The students had all been saying it behind his back for a long time, and he had probably heard them. The teacher lost his temper and screamed at the kid to shut up. The kid threw his uncapped Magic Marker at the teacher and a green streak ran across the teacher's cheek. All the students were holding markers, which, in mounting excitement, they began to throw. By the time he fled the room, the teacher had marks on his tie, his white shirt, and the arm he had thrown up to cover his face. "Can you believe that he cried?" one of my students asked with still-fresh amazement.

A Union soldier serving in the South said of the freedman, "Human or not, there he is in our midst, millions strong; and if he is not educated mentally and morally, he will make us trouble." That, in short, is the theory on which our public school system is based. By 1880 it had already developed its fundamental characteristics—it was, and is, as Michael Katz writes, "universal, tax-supported, free, compulsory, bureaucratic, racist, and class-biased."

The first school dedicated to the education of freed slaves was a modified plantation. Missionaries took over management of the plantation, overseeing freedmen who continued to work the same fields they had worked under slavery. The freedmen were compensated for their labor with food, clothing, housing, and lessons limited to basic memorization. Believing that "the untrained mind of generations will reveal its weakness just where the higher faculties begin to come into existence," the missionaries focused their instruction on the importance of matrimony, hygiene, honesty, and sobriety. Later, primers written specifically for freedmen's schools would emphasize the values Northerners wanted to instill in this new workforce. Spelling words would include themes like "kneel," "clean," and "scrub."

"Miss Eula is ashamed of this entire class, and ashamed to be your teacher," is how I began the speech I made the day after one of my students refused to come to class because all the other kids were calling him gay. I told the students to make a list of all the names they had ever been called, good and bad, and to write about one of the worst names.

Vanessalee wrote: "Shorty, Tweety, Devil, Crazy, Perky, Evil, Pretty, Porky, Piggy, Miss Piggy, Jerk, Fool, Stupid, Bitch, Ugly. When my friends call me Porky, Pork, Miss Piggy, Porky Pig, Pig I feel bad at times but other times I know that they are playing with me."

Shamel wrote: "Ghetto Indian, Sham, Marshmello, Jagup, Mr. Scientist, Homo, Bitch, Dick, Retard, YoYo. One time I was in class and this boy called me Soy Coke. I was very mad. Then after that day everyone started to call me that. I was getting very tired. I never did like that name, so I hope he turns into a rat."

Ricky wrote: "Sonny, Smarty Pants, Roach, Big Head, Fucking Bitch, Dick, Spic. A bad name someone had ever called me in my life was The Roach because every one thought I went out with this girl named The Roach but I had never went out with her. But then they stopped the other day. Another bad name someone had ever called me was Spic but I don't really care because I know the person is playing with me and when he gets on my nerves I call him Hamburger Helper. His name is Rajick."

"How is Ricky getting called a spic like Michael getting called a faggot?" I asked.

Silence. "It's not," Shamel suggested. "Being gay is different than being Latino." True. My lesson plan, I realized, was flawed. It was also designed to manipulate how my students thought. I wanted to make them more liberal-minded—I wanted to make them think like me. With discomfort, I recalled my supervisor informing us that our goal should be not only to teach our students writing, but to make them "better people."

I was not a regular classroom teacher in New York, a fact for which I was always grateful, but a stopgap creative writing teacher working short shifts in two schools in the Bronx and one in Harlem. One of the schools in the Bronx had a very large, echoing cafeteria that functioned during several points throughout the day as a kind of giant holding pen for students. The other had road cones out in the street, in between which the students were allowed to stand for ten minutes after lunch. There was a gym in that school, but no gym teacher, so there was no gym class, and no art class, no music class—no subjects, in fact, that were not tested by the state. The school in Harlem where I spent most of my time had wire mesh over the windows and in the stairwells. When the students walked through it, slapping the walls and dragging their feet, the whole place rattled like a cage.

I lost, in those buildings, all the easy answers I had ever heard put to the problems of schools, but I still persisted in believing that there had to be a better way to educate children. What that way might be eluded me more fully the longer I stayed, and the possibilities ceased very quickly to seem as endless as they had during my training, when I had studied educational theory. The public school system, I discovered, defied theory. And this system, I became convinced, rendered individuals impotent.

Stories were always circulating through those schools about teachers who had not been able to "take it." There was the teacher who tried to throw a kid out a window, there was the teacher who beat his first graders with a broom handle, and there was the teacher, the one I happened to know, who told his class to "shut the fuck up, you little fuckers."

Judging from the terms in which they spoke, Northerners did not seem to believe that freed slaves needed to be educated so much as they needed to be taught a lesson. Shortly after emancipation, the *New York Times* argued against giving land to freedmen, on the grounds that the former slaves should first be instructed in hard work, patience, and frugality. Centuries of slavery, apparently, had not sufficiently provided those lessons.

Nearly two hundred thousand black soldiers had served in the Union Army, and by the end of the war one-third of them were missing or dead. Forty thousand black farmers had been granted "possessory titles" to large sections of South Carolina and Georgia during the war. But after the war, when Johnson pardoned the planters who had owned that land, those titles became meaningless. And then the Freedman's Bank failed, losing the first savings of the freed slaves.

Most of us learn as children to doubt the promises of adults. And we become either bold or wary as we discover what the world truly has to offer us. "By the way," a child of the bold variety once said to me casually, as he led me into his backyard to play, "watch out for land mines."

I was asked one morning on my way into the school in Harlem to lecture a student on the importance of attendance. The student stared on sullenly as I glanced over her attendance record, which was handed to me by a busy secretary. Considering the circumstances, I didn't think it looked very bad. The secretary had no way of knowing that I myself had avoided school as often as possible when I was young. I used hot water to elevate my temperature and jumping jacks to bring on sweats, and then I complained of dizziness and ringing in my ears, symptoms so odd that my parents didn't doubt I was ill. Because of my absences, I never fully learned my multiplication tables, I never learned to write in cursive, and I did not learn, until high school, any more of American history than that the North was good and the South was bad.

Until I finally resigned myself to my education in sixth grade, I did everything I could to avoid it, despite the fact that my teachers did not, for the most part, chronically underestimate me or openly despise me. So I found it difficult now, as a teacher, to think of anything to say to the student standing in front of me. I recognized another passive resister when I saw one, and I respected her tactics.

The principal of that school would, at some point that year, ask me into her office to discuss my use of the word "vagina" in an after-school class for teenaged girls. Discovering with dismay that I was still, nearly two decades after my truancy, afraid of principals and their power, I would suggest that there was nothing inherently dirty about the word and that if the girls were not already familiar with this term, they ought to be. "I know that," the principal would say impatiently, rolling her eyes, "but the parents don't."

Many of the teachers I worked with tended to regard the parents of their students with either pity or contempt. These parents, I was reminded on many occasions, were neglectful, or addicted, or abusive, or simply ignorant. Undoubtedly, some of these things were true, as they are true of many parents. But what is striking to me now is how closely this portrait of parents resembles the way Northerners once imagined freed slaves: as indolent, simple, intemperate, and prone to violence.

I didn't have occasion to meet many of the parents of my students, but the teenaged girls with whom I used the word "vagina" staged a performance in which they spoke in the voices of their own grandmothers and mothers. The women they brought to the stage were far more human, of course, than any of the specters conjured in school. There was Chanita, articulate and wary and self-possessed, speaking as her Polish grandmother who married a Puerto Rican man and learned Spanish and raised her children in Harlem, where she was twice a stranger. And then there was Marisol, funny and confident and overdramatic, speaking as her stubborn mother and ending her monologue on hardship with a song from church, dropping to her knees on the stage, holding her cupped hands out in front of her, and singing, full-voice, "Fill my cup, Lord, I offer up my cup, Lord. . . ."

Being afraid of children is not, in itself, much of a crime. It is more of an indignity. But disguising the fearful things we do to children as essential elements of their education is as good as dynamiting the foundation of the classroom. The walls are bound to collapse, eventually, around that betrayal, and bring with them the roof. One of the most frightening things about children, in my experience, is their intelligence. They inevitably know more than we suspect them of knowing. They appraise us with devastating accuracy. And they are aware of injustices we have learned to ignore.

During my first year of teaching, I found that I said "Quiet!" more than anything else. I did not exactly fear my students so much as I dreaded their insurrections, but I am sure that distinction did not make much difference to them. I dreaded their insurrections because I suspected that the quality of my teaching would be judged by my ability to control my students. I often heard other teachers using terms like "classroom management," "reinforcement," and "discipline." Surprisingly, "empowerment" was also popular. The teachers I worked with misused the term "empowerment" all the time. They developed "empowering" exercises like letting the students draft their own rules, but the rules were always the same. True empowerment of students, I came to realize, necessarily means a certain disempowerment of teachers.

During Reconstruction, Radical Republicans made proposals that might have granted freed slaves some meaningful power. But both presidents Lincoln and Johnson favored a plan for Reconstruction that avoided questions of social and political power in favor of education. This left the freedmen to discover that, as Ronald Butchart writes, "although some individuals have been able to exploit formal instruction for their personal intellectual emancipation, education alone has probably never been liberating for a group, social class, or race, when its ends, method, and curriculum have been defined and controlled by others."

I half expected, for some time, that the dark spot would disappear if I closed one eye. And so I would find myself sitting in an empty math classroom feeling vaguely unsettled and staring at a sign that read, "Caring means learning the terms and remembering them." Other signs in those schools reminded me of the chapters of Isaac Brinckerhoff's 1864 *Advice to Freedmen:* "Be Industrious," "Be Economical," "Be Temperate," and "Be Soldiers."

On a September morning in my second year of teaching, I stood at the back door of the school in Harlem with a janitor who was telling me that he, being from Ireland, had seen some terrorism in his time and didn't like it. The only acts of terrorism I had witnessed up until that day were the harmless but significant rebellions of schoolchildren—the refusals to speak, the refusals to be quiet, the uncapped markers thrown at the teacher's face—and I was very close to having lost my willingness to quell such rebellions. It would take me only until the end of that school year to decide that I did not have the stomach for what went on in schools where children were herded from one subjugation to another.

On that morning the panicked voice of a reporter on the radio in the school office told us that a thick black cloud was engulfing the city and that it looked like nothing he had ever seen, like a mushroom cloud, like Hiroshima. I would later stare out of my window in Queens at the distant plume of smoke in Manhattan and the planeless sky and dwell on the grave inaccuracy of that comparison, but at the moment I didn't yet know that an atom bomb had not been dropped on the city. Even so, I was calm, because I suspected Harlem was far from anything that mattered to most of the world, and too close to ruin to bother destroying. The principal ordered us not to let the students out of the school, and I was told to guard the back door with the janitor, who had put a mop through the door handles to prevent them from opening in either direction. It was for the good of the students, I knew, that we were keeping them in the school, but standing at that locked door was emblematic to me of who I really was as a teacher.

Goodbye to All That

For me, New York ended as soon as it began. The day I moved into my first apartment, I discovered that the reason the kitchen had looked so big was that there was no refrigerator. I also discovered that water didn't flow out of any of the taps. Sal, the plumber who scolded me for letting him in before I asked if he was the plumber, stood in the doorway to my bedroom after he fixed the sinks. I was staring at a wall, holding a paintbrush and a can of paint. He asked, "Did they teach you to paint like that in college?"

So Sal painted my room while I listened to the story of his life and the story of my neighborhood. It had been Finnish when Sal moved there from Sicily as a young boy, and then it was Italian, and then Jewish, and now it was Puerto Rican. After he finished painting my room, Sal drove around looking for used refrigerators, found one, fixed it, put it on my front stoop, rang the bell, and drove away. By the time I got downstairs, the refrigerator had already been stolen.

But that is not the way it really happened. That is how I

learned to tell the story of my life in New York. I learned to make my experience of being young and new to the city sound effortless and zany. It was not.

I didn't mention that I couldn't go down to get the refrigerator Sal found because it was impossible for me to carry it up four flights of stairs alone. It was taken only after I left it on the stoop for an entire day while I tried to think of someone I could ask for help. I didn't mention the animal-piss stink of my room or the extreme aching sense of helplessness that overcame me when I realized that I would have to buy a refrigerator. I didn't mention that I couldn't hear out of my right ear because it became clogged from crying. I didn't mention all the time I wasted in bed, staring at the ceiling, debilitated with dread. Or the time I wasted trying to find out if landlords were required to provide refrigerators in units over a certain size. Or the call to my landlord, when he laughed at me, saying, "Look, either you take the place as it is, or you find somewhere else to live." I didn't mention hurting my hand when I punched the door frame in frustration. Or my sickening realization that Sal was helping me because I was white. He made me aware of this fact with a barrage of racial slurs that I failed to respond to with anything but silence. Silence because I needed his help and I suddenly understood the contract.

"You gotta get a better lock on that door," Sal advised. I pointed out that I didn't own anything except a bed. "Yeah, well these Puerto Ricans will steal that bed right out from under you," he said. Silence.

I ran into Sal once more before I left the city. He was getting into a car in Brooklyn's Chinatown with his daughter, who was not white at all. Sal, like everyone else in New York, was not exactly who the story might lead you to believe he was.

I hardly even knew the story back then—I had only a vague sense that the heroine was young and that the moral had something to do with being in the right place at the right time. I was ready for anything. I moved to the city during a record heat wave and calmly braced myself for an entire summer of filling the bathtub with ice cubes to cool my body at night. But it was never again that hot in New York. And I learned every detail of the story just as fast as I discovered its falsehood.

I remember a moment from my first days in the city when I was lost in Brooklyn somewhere around Avenue J. Sweat was trickling over my breastbone and the sun was burning my scalp. I couldn't identify the exact nature of any of the businesses I was walking past, but they seemed to deal in car parts. Dozens of taillights in all different sizes and shades of red hung, sparkling, from chain-link fences. Suddenly, I felt a desperate need to call my mother. I tried three pay phones and lost five quarters before I found one that worked. When I got her on the line, all I could do was lean against the searing metal phone booth and sob.

Not that I wasn't dazzled by the city. Every nerve in my body was electrified by New York. I was on an endless sidewalk surrounded by bare bulbs and whistles and sudden flocks of pigeons and huge fading stretches of concrete. I believe that I will never feel like that again—so raw and so moved.

I was always lost in New York, even after I stopped walking east when I intended to walk west. There were just ways in which I fundamentally did not know where I was. I grew up north of the city, in the Hudson River Valley. But the water that flowed through upstate New York might as well have been a different substance from the water that flowed into New York Harbor. Where I came from, the river smelled distinctly of crayfish and grew a leafy skin in the summer. In the winter the ice groaned and cracked under the weight of all the surrounding silence. I would not have had any trouble believing, when I arrived in New York, that the water in the harbor had all been brought in on barges. Everything about the city seemed at least that absurd.

I was naive enough then to imagine that living a few blocks from the harbor would be pleasant. And I was innocent enough not to know that I should not walk down the street carrying two melons in my arms at about the level of my chest—even if melons were two for a dollar. From the roof of my building in Brooklyn I could see giant barges silhouetted against the hazy pink horizon at dusk. I tried to walk down to the water and promptly dead-ended at a huge, windowless building labeled Terminal Warehouse. On my way back, a bus driver at a red light yelled to me that I shouldn't be walking around down there. I got on the bus just to humor him and rode past train yards bordered with barbed wire. Then I took a train to Coney Island.

The station at Coney Island was half-charred from a fire decades ago and packed with giant inflatable pink seals for sale. An abandoned wooden box read, "The world's tiniest horse!" Caramel apples were seventy-five cents and the din of the fair games was intolerable. One freak-show announcer screamed, "If you love your family, you will take them to see the two-headed baby!" It was gross and crazy and base—it was everything I would ever love about the city. The beach was packed with naked flesh and smelled like beer and mango. And the Wonder Wheel inspired real wonder as I rose up over Brooklyn in a swinging metal cage.

Did I know it would all cost something sooner or later? All the bewilderment and disorientation? I'm not sure. But I remember the moment when I realized exactly what it had already cost me. A friend and I thought it would be fun to go ice-skating in Prospect Park, but, like most things in New York that are supposed to be fun, it was miserable. The rented skates were as dull as spoons, the ice was slush, and it was so crowded that all we could do was keep ourselves standing and try to avoid being burned by cigarettes while we were pushed and shoved in a slow circle. We had both been very good ice-skaters as children.

I arrived in New York at twenty-one, with a poor sense of direction and a worse sense of time. I set my watch first five minutes fast, then ten, then fifteen. I was only going to stay six months. I stayed three years, and I never stopped thinking about leaving. But when I left, I left my entire life behind. I have to explain to you why I no longer live in New York, but first I have to explain to myself why I stayed so long. Because what I want to say about living there is that it is not, as the mythology goes, more real than anyplace else. In some ways, it is less.

I noticed during my time in New York that many of the people I met there had a habit of describing how miserable they were, then arguing that they couldn't leave the city because it was so wonderful. When someone who spends the better part of every day in a cubicle and only occasionally makes it out to sit in a loud, dull bar tells me that she is living in the city for "the pace, the excitement, the culture, the—you know—stimulation," I have trouble fully believing her.

The myth of New York seems to be sustained by the fact that so many people who live there are from somewhere else. They come to the city and immediately dedicate themselves to making it the city of their imagination. The—you know—glittering city of endless opportunity that oozes riches and delights for the young and talented. I also came from somewhere else. Somewhere not far away but so clearly foreign that people often asked what country I was from. I always felt like an expatriate in the city, and I came knowing just a few of the stories that everyone has been told.

By now I consider almost everything that is often said about New York to be false. To begin with, the city is not that big or that worldly. An astonishing number of people who live there rarely leave their borough, let alone the country. And if you are part of the elite, as Joan Didion found, New York is like a small town. A tiny population of New York is rich or famous, and much of the rest of the city is in service to that population. For most people, even the elite, it is a city of drudgery. You sweat in the hot station, then you shiver in the crowded train, then you walk for ten blocks without an umbrella through a pounding summer thunderstorm . . . and you do this with desperation, because you have no other obvious choice. You do it every day. There is a series of statements on the supporting beams of one of the tunnels under Forty-second Street that reads:

Overslept,
so tired.
If late,
get fired.
Why bother?
Why the pain?
Just go home
do it again.

Those words always affected me, although I never worked
long enough at any one job to fully understand that particular
brand of drudgery. I read them as words of caution. My work in
New York was, like the work of everyone else I knew, whatever
I could find. I watered plants in the offices of *TV Guide* at one
point, I cleaned a bookstore twice a week for a while, I was a
waitress for a few days, I did inspections of community gardens
under the parks department for quite some time, I proofread
just long enough to learn proofreaders' marks, I did transcrip-
tions now and then, I opened mail, I taught writing for a couple
of years, I temped, and I was briefly an editorial assistant at a
major publishing house. My job as an editorial assistant was by
far the most menial work I ever did in the city. I remember it
mostly as a series of pointless trips in elevators. And I remember the way my friend described a similar job: "I professionally
destroy paper clips."

But I still believed in the mystical power of the city to trans-
form me into a writer—a real writer. I wasn't sure exactly how
this alchemy would happen, which is one reason I kept changing jobs, but I was convinced that just living in the city could

make my writing more legitimate. By the time I left New York, I had learned that the distinction between a writer and a real writer is superficial. And I suddenly understood the advice that more established writers had been giving me all along. "Move somewhere else—anywhere else," one journalist had recommended soon after I moved to New York. "Pick any other city."

There is a popular legend of New York as the gritty city of hard knocks and rough neighborhoods and real danger and police chases and wild nights. I suppose that watching a bum with no legs being dragged out of his stinking pile of blankets by four policemen is gritty, but it lacks any of the dirty romance implied by the word. Standing for an entire day in a clinic crowded with sick babies and pregnant women because you don't have health insurance and you've been ill for several months also lacks romance. So does spending hours on the telephone, waiting for the chance to explain that you were billed twice for the month of June. One of my most vivid memories from that first year in New York is the smell of the oil soap I always used to clean my floors. While I was on hold with the telephone company or the gas company or the credit-card company, I would sit on the floor, examining the splinters in the wood and inhaling the strange scent of oil soap.

Not even the dangers of New York are what the story dictates. I was harassed by children nearly as often as I was harassed by men in the city. I remember smiling at an eight-year-old boy on the train who stared at me stonily before he half closed his eyes and slowly ran his tongue across his upper lip as he fingered his crotch. While I was working for the parks department, I spent most of my time in neighborhoods imagined as "rough," where one or two people might ask me if I was lost. Often I *was* lost, and I got directions that were usually wrong from people who were always nice. The worst thing I was ever threatened with in New York was a lighter. And it was terrifying. But the man standing in the middle of the sidewalk in front of me, flicking his lighter, didn't hurt me. He stared at me and said softly, "How ya doing, princess?" I told him that I had been working all day and that I was very tired, and he said he knew how I felt and walked away.

I often woke before dawn and could not fall back to sleep. I lay there listening to the car alarms cycle through all their different sounds while my heart raced for no reason. It is hard for me to separate my experience of living in New York from the sensation of reaching the limits of my own independence. I was excruciatingly lonely, and everything was unfamiliar and difficult. But, in a way, I was living my dream. Long after I discarded every illusion I ever had about New York, I still treasured the empty fantasy of complete autonomy.

If I had entertained more illusions, I might have been able to stay in New York longer. I might have even considered myself happier. But I was not tickled by the daily opportunity to change trains in Rockefeller Center, I did not feel lucky to be surrounded by merchandise I couldn't afford, and I had absolutely no interest in the nightlife, whatever that is.

I didn't participate in the New York of the collective imagination, which may be one reason that I don't believe in it. My interactions with people I didn't know were always brief and often painful. One afternoon I crashed my bike into a man just as he stepped off the curb in Chinatown. Our heads slammed together, and I fell onto the sidewalk. For an instant I lay there, looking up at an advertisement for Asian escorts on the side of a building, smelling the reek of the fish market and listening to the humming motor of a tiny scuba diver who swam in a wash-tub next to me. The man I had hit was holding his forehead and seemed to be getting more and more agitated as people with orange bags of bok choy crowded around me to make sure I was all right while they left him standing alone. Scared and still see-ing a few swimming lights from the impact, I got onto my bike quickly and rode away. I stopped after a few blocks and cried hysterically in dismay. No one looked at me. In ways I find hard to explain, most of the interactions I had in New York were like this one. Which may be why I always felt more comfortable simply observing other people's lives.

I watched everything carefully and never quite lost the con-viction that I was missing something. *So, what's so good about all this?* I kept thinking. I suspected that there was a secret I hadn't been told. I was convinced that I had only one chance to do the right things and meet the right people and that I would surely fail. Everything was irrevocable, and nothing was within reach. The peculiar paralysis I felt when I first came to the city was mostly from the sense that every decision I made would last the rest of my life. I know now that I was right and I was wrong. Success and failure were the terms in which young people who had just moved to the city spoke. It was not a place to live as much as it was a test or a game. I despise both. "Why don't you leave?" I asked people endlessly, even though I could not yet ex-plain why I didn't leave. "Because I don't want to admit that I failed," one friend said. "Because I have to prove to myself that I can do this." By the time I left New York, I knew that success and failure are silly terms in which to speak of living a life.

I read Joan Didion's essay "Goodbye to All That" before I ever saw the trenches of New York. All I remember of that first reading is that I didn't like the title. I knew nothing at all back then. I did not know that I would return to that essay again and again, and that I would eventually feel compelled to rewrite it.

But I remember, distinctly, walking down Fourth Avenue in Brooklyn for the first time, past the car wash and the huge windowless warehouses and the brick buildings bristling with TV antennas and the billboard that read, "Se Hacen." I looked around and thought, with wonder, *I'm going to love all this someday.* And I did.

Still, I feel jarred by "I ♥ NY" bumper stickers and repulsed by "I ♥ NY" T-shirts. Especially now that the slogan has become so grossly fetishized, like the flag. I don't want the New York I loved to be confused with the New York the T-shirts love. That isn't the same city. I didn't love the *New Yorker's* New York or the New York of the *New York Times.* I didn't love Joan Didion's New York, or anyone else's fantasy of the place. I loved my own experience of the city, which was rarely what I expected it to be. I loved the people I knew there, who were unlike any character in any TV show or movie set in New York that I have ever seen. I was most comfortable with people for whom New York was not a mirage, and I most trusted people who hated it there.

New York took everything I had. I moved four times, and each time I owned less. I left New York without even a bed. I no longer had potted plants, or framed pieces of art, or a snapshot of my father. I remember the moment when I threw that snapshot out. I was sifting through my things before another hurried move with a borrowed car, and I looked at the photo, thinking, *I don't really need this—he still looks almost the same.* That was just before I noticed that my father had gone gray.

In New York, even one snapshot became too much of a burden to carry from one place to another. The mementos of my childhood began to weigh like lead. And so did my adolescent preoccupation with the real. Like many young people who go to college immediately after high school, I had learned to talk about the real world as if it were in an entirely different universe from the one I lived in. With the blind enthusiasm and embarrassing ignorance of a colonial explorer, I left college determined to discover the real world. I didn't just want to live there—I wanted to be made real myself. This might be the saddest part of my story, because New York did not make me feel more legitimate or real. Actually, it made me feel as if I barely existed. As I wandered through the surprisingly solid streets of that mostly fictitious city, people often bumped into me very hard, as if I were invisible. Now I agree with my grandmother, who recently said, "The real question is—what is authenticity, anyway?"

For most of my time in New York, I lived in Brooklyn and worked in Harlem. I considered this a clever evasion of The City. Where I lived was just a place to live, not The Place. And where I worked was just a place to work, not The Place. I rode my bike to work early in the morning, when even the streets of Midtown were still empty. I rattled over the Brooklyn Bridge, looking down through the wooden slats at the water below. I swerved through Chinatown. And then I rode up Mulberry Street, through Little Italy, where the street carnival had been the night before. The strings of lights were still hanging, but not illuminated. The cobblestones were covered with trash. And the sausage vendor was asleep at the wooden counter with his head resting on his folded arms.

The New York I knew was always the city of the morning after the carnival. I rode all the way uptown on First Avenue, from Little Italy to Harlem. I walked from 110th to 140th, from Frederick Douglass to Martin Luther King Jr. Boulevard. I passed murals painted on the boards that covered the broken windows of the old brownstones—the Virgin Mary on one window, St. Lazarus, with his crutches and his dog, on the other. I read the messages chalked onto the sidewalk by De La Vega every morning: "You are more desirable as a servant of the machine than as a free thinker." I saw the glorious graffiti on the basketball courts. I stepped over dog shit. I watched the Eastern European woman who worked in the pizza shop grow thin and develop a sore on her face while the boys from the school came in and yelled at her to hurry up with that slice, bitch. I glared at the boys and they didn't meet my eyes. Almost no one did. I listened to the guys in the bodega betting on the Mets and laughing. I smiled at babies in strollers. I watched kids on bikes ride through traffic and pop up onto their back wheels. Sometimes I ate in the hospital café, because it was the only place I knew I could get spinach for lunch. I watched women in hot, hot dresses, and I watched the men watching them. I listened to Rosie, the police officer, singing Aretha Franklin in the bathroom of the school where I worked. I knew, intimately, the empty lots where grandmas from Alabama grew okra and collard greens. I found a cat that had drowned in a rain barrel and was gathering mold. At the bodega on First Avenue I saw the old man who was always trying to remember my name. "Ida!" he would jump up and yell, "Ursula, Ursula, Ursula!"

This was the New York I loved, with the imperfect, ambiguous, hesitant love that I have come to recognize as my own. It was the city that existed on the margins of the story. It was the New York of Harlem and Inwood and Washington Heights. The New York of the outer boroughs. The New York of Brooklyn and Queens and Staten Island and the Bronx.

But see, the name of every place in New York serves as a code word or a racial cue. The code shifts slightly, depending on whom you are talking to, so that at times the word "Harlem" will mean "dangerous" and "tough" and at other times will mean "vibrant" and "real." But it is always a setting for our same old stories. What an injustice to a place. A place that is, incidentally, real. When I moved to New York, I had the luxury at first of living in a neighborhood that most of the people I met had never heard of. Sunset Park meant nothing. But Fort Greene did, and so did Astoria, and the East Village meant so much that I tried to avoid admitting I lived there. "It's temporary," I would say. But so was everything.

My friends often say, "When you come back to New York . . . ," assuming, of course, that I will come back. And maybe I will, despite it all. Joan Didion did. But for now I prefer to think that I will go somewhere that is not so overimagined.

I lived in the city just long enough to see Coney Island begin to be destroyed. The spring I left New York was the same spring I discovered that the old vine-covered roller coaster had finally been torn down. So had the ancient candy shop with the home-made caramel apples. And the burned train station was being renovated.

It has been said that New York is a city for only the very rich and the very poor. Joan Didion suggested that it is a city for only the very young. In my worst moments, especially when standing on Madison Avenue, I have suspected that it is a city for only the very desperate or the very deluded.

I have at times been mystified by Joan Didion's ability to tolerate certain myths while she so fiercely and effectively destroys the foundations of many others. But I know now that it is very difficult to dismantle one story without replacing it with another. The romance of narrative is so hard to resist. Like Joan Didion, I made a yellow curtain for my first bedroom in the city because I had a romantic notion of light and color. My curtain also became grimy in the rain.

It is not that the heroine is no longer as optimistic as she once was. It is that the heroine is not convinced she is the heroine or that the story is true. The heroine knows that New York is just a city—just a place to live. And, like any other place, it demands that you make your own story.

I came to New York very young, and I left still young but not the same. The Wonder Wheel is still there, true, but everything else is gone.

California

Black News

The news was the same in California as it had been in New York. The *New York Times* was reporting that Iraq would allow UN weapons inspectors to return but that Bush did not want to wait for the inspectors to do their work. The *Los Angeles Times* was reporting that Bush planned to tell the UN that the United States would act on Iraq if the UN did not. The term "pre-emptive strike" had been in the air for some time, and it seemed inevitable, already, that we would go to war. None of this was new, and none of it was news, really.

In San Diego, I was surprised by how much the beaches resembled advertisements for beaches. The surf was rougher and the sand was coarser than it looked in travel brochures, but most of the people on Pacific Beach were young and white and tanned and muscular. Because the first place I went in San Diego was the beach, my initial assessment of the city was that it was almost entirely white. I would realize later that going to the beach in San Diego is like going to Wall Street in New York. It is not only a center of elite commerce—it is a place where the city's imagination of itself resides. And I would begin to understand that the city of San Diego imagines its beaches white by telling itself the same story over and over, which is also how some of us, when we read the *New York Times,* convince ourselves that this is The News.

I did not live near the beach in San Diego. I lived in a neighborhood where some houses had grass on their lawns and others had gravel. There were four liquor stores within two blocks of my apartment. Ten blocks away, there was a bus stop, and across from the bus stop was a battered plastic box that was filled every week with an African American community newspaper, the *San Diego Voice and Viewpoint.* I had never noticed this box, and I had never read the paper, until I was hired by the *Voice and Viewpoint* as a part-time reporter and photographer.

My first assignment was to cover an event involving a city-council seat. I went directly from my job interview to my first assignment with a map and a borrowed camera. During the course of that event, where I was the only white person in attendance, I learned the word "infrastructure" and the fact that District Four was important. District Four, I gleaned, was where black folks lived in San Diego.

"What are the boundaries of District Four?" I asked the candidate for city council after his speech. "What?" he asked, and squinted at me like I was shiny. "I'm new in town," I said, to explain my ignorance, "and I'm wondering what areas are included in District Four, what neighborhoods."

"Oh, I don't know, honey," he said, suddenly disinterested, and then yelled across the room, to a woman who was at the door, getting ready to leave, "Hey, this girl want to know where it safe for her to go."

In my first few weeks at the *Voice and Viewpoint,* I covered the possible jury misconduct in the conviction of a particularly big black man who did not match the description of any of the witnesses in his case. And I covered the swearing-in of the postmaster of Chula Vista, who remarked, "We used to say, 'Through rain or snow or sleet'—now we say, 'Through anthrax or pipe bombs or snipers.'" I covered the weekly meetings of the Catfish Club, a thirty-two-year-old gathering of community leaders formerly known as the Colored Folk Club. I covered the efforts of the Black Chamber of Commerce to reach out to the Hispanic community. I covered a San Diego that did not appear in the travel brochures. This San Diego was not concerned with the surf report. This San Diego was concerned with its infrastructure, with working streetlights, school-building repair, and extending the public-transportation service.

The front-page story the week that I was hired at the *Voice* was about a San Diego woman whose four-day-old baby had been taken by Child Protective Services and not returned, even after the woman had divorced her abusive husband, who was then deported. Also on the front page was an AP story about black farmers protesting discriminatory farm-loan practices by the Farm Services Agency. And an AP story about how the wife of Alex Haley, author of *Roots,* lost the rights to his estate after his death. The next week's front page would report on a study finding that more black men were now incarcerated than were enrolled in colleges or universities. In 1980, the study noted, three times more black men had been enrolled in institutions of higher learning than had been behind bars.

Along with an article about Pastor Cooper's sixtieth wedding anniversary and a full-page spread of Aunt Sarah's 104th-birthday party, the *Voice and Viewpoint* ran articles about the 2002 conviction of two white men in the murder of a black woman during a 1969 race riot, about members of the old Black Panther Party condemning the new Black Panther Party as racist and anti-Semitic, and about U.S. interest in African oil reserves. While newspapers all over the country were covering the DC-area sniper, the *Voice* ran a Black Press of America editorial headlined, "Do Black Suspected Snipers Stigmatize the Entire Race?"

And while the *New York Times* reported on September 11 memorial ceremonies in Sacramento, Kansas, Seattle, Fresno, and Decatur under the headline "A Single Grief Knits Together a Vast Country," the *Voice and Viewpoint* picked up a Black Press of America article with the headline "9/11 Did Not Cure Racism," in which the president of the Detroit NAACP wrote, "The fact that we have known terror and there's still no legitimate move to address the domestic terror that's visited upon African-Americans and people of color . . . leaves a void among the races."

It wasn't a distinctly different telling of the news that made reading the *Voice and Viewpoint* so unlike reading any other newspaper. Many of the stories reprinted there had already appeared as AP stories or Black Press of America stories in papers all over the country, but it was the effect they had when they appeared all together, as a collection of Black News, that was alarming. It was in the word "another," which appeared in every headline the paper ran about children taken from their families by Child Protective Services: "Another Mother Suffers the Nightmare of CPS," and, "Child Protective Services Fails Another Family," and, "The Child Protection Agency Forces Another Family Apart."

When I was not the only white person at the events I covered for the *Voice,* the other white person was usually a politician. Once I arrived at a speech by a candidate for state assembly, Vince Hall, and sat down at a table next to an elderly man who looked at me, looked at my camera, looked at Vince Hall, and asked me, with a tilt of his head, "You related to him?"

When I talk about my family to strangers, I occasionally describe it as mixed. Because I don't appear to be of mixed race, this term usually confuses people. What I mean is not specifically that my mother's sister married a black man from Jamaica and had two children, and that one of these cousins came to live with my family when I was in junior high, and that I lived with the other cousin in Brooklyn after I graduated from college. And I don't mean specifically that my mother's sister later remarried and adopted a black son, or that my mother's other sister adopted a Cherokee daughter. And I don't mean specifically that my mother lived with a black man after her divorce from my father, and that his daughter lived with us as my stepsister, and that later, when my stepsister lost custody of her baby, my mother raised the baby for some time. And I don't mean specifically that my mother later married a man from

China, and that his daughter is now another sister in my family. What I mean is all of this. And what I said to the man who asked me if I was related to the other white person in the room was, "As much as you are."

When I was sixteen, my mother's boyfriend Barry told me, with frustration, "We have cultural differences," but that phrase meant nothing to me then. I remember puzzling over it briefly and then discarding it as meaningless. At that moment, Barry and I were having an argument about whether or not Barry should spank my brother, and my position was that, cultural differences or not, nobody was going to touch my little brother.

I would remember that moment when I interviewed a woman named Eve Johnson for my first story involving Child Protective Services. Because she had already written several letters to the paper, I knew some of her story already. I knew that Child Protective Services had taken her grandchildren away from her daughter-in-law because her daughter-in-law's new boyfriend had been abusing them. I knew that the children were two and five years old. And I knew that the children had been placed in foster care, despite the fact that Ms. Johnson wanted to care for them.

What I would learn, when she came to my office, was that Ms. Johnson had a certificate in early-childhood education. She had served as a teacher's aide for seven years. She had also, by the time I spoke with her, completed a series of workshops for prospective foster parents. After learning the requirements for certification as a foster parent, Ms. Johnson told me, she had been surprised that she did not already have the children. "I'm active, I cook, I have time to give, I babysit for friends," she told me. "There's no reason why I shouldn't be caring for those kids."

When she first requested that her grandchildren be placed with her, two weeks after they were taken from their mother, Ms. Johnson was required to have a fingerprint scan and a background check. The fingerprint scan revealed that Ms. Johnson had been convicted of the felony "discharging a firearm with gross negligence" in 1989. From that point forward, this would be the fact around which her entire case revolved. It would also be the fact that interested me least. At some point I reluctantly asked Ms. Johnson why she discharged that firearm, but the extent to which I felt that it was none of my business is reflected by the omission of her answer in my notes. I made only the vague notation "Domestic violence," which I do not now know how to interpret.

To me, the gun was not the story. This was in part because the crime had already been punished. Ms. Johnson had served her probation without incident, and her sentence did not include any restrictions on raising her grandchildren. But, more important, I was beginning to understand that the gun in Ms. Johnson's story was functioning, again and again, as an excuse for the inexcusable. And after working my way through the file of letters that had been sent to the *Voice* by parents whose children had been taken away by Child Protective Services, and after doing some more interviews, I was beginning to understand that there was always a gun, there was always a crime that was being punished, no matter how far outside the law the punishment was ranging.

In the case of Tonya, a young mother who asked me not to print her last name, the gun was a fistfight with her sister. Tonya's mother had called the police to break up this fight, and the police officer who responded had called in a social worker because Tonya had two small children. The social worker took Tonya's two-week-old infant and her toddler because she mistook the birthmarks on the infant's back and bottom for bruises. "It was like an abduction," Tonya told me. A child-abuse expert later identified the bruises on Tonya's baby as permanent birthmarks, but the baby and his brother were not returned. After seven months of taking mandated classes and appearing in court and dealing with first one social worker and then another, Tonya still did not have her children, for reasons that were entirely obscure.

I wasn't unfamiliar with child-protection agencies, or their services, when I began working for the *Voice.* My stepsister had a baby a few years after I left home for college, and when her baby was around a year old, she got drunk and passed out long enough for the baby to start wailing and for her landlord to call the police, who arrested her for endangering a child. The New York State Office of Children and Family Services took the baby, and for some time my mother and Barry cared for her. This would have been all right if Barry hadn't been in the process of losing his mind, a process that had started very quietly but was just then reaching a crescendo. He was, during that time, screaming at my mother and then pulling the phone out of the wall when she tried to use it. I had left some potted plants with my mother when I moved out, and when I came back for them the pots were smashed. Back then, when the baby was passed on to another relative, I was relieved.

And that's the story the papers liked to cover. When the *San*

Diego Union-Tribune covered stories about Child Protective Services, they tended to cover the story of a father who beat his infant to death, or the story of a mother who tried to stuff her toddler into a trash can outside Taco Bell. These stories occasionally carried an implicit criticism of CPS for not acting faster and for not taking children away from their parents sooner. But they never suggested that CPS might be systematically removing black children from their family networks and that, in light of America's history of eugenics, this might be problematic. Perhaps now that we believe nurture plays at least as much a part in child development as nature, we simply take children away from black women instead of sterilizing them. At the time that this thought occurred to me, I did not know that African American parents are much more likely to be investigated for abuse and neglect than parents of any other racial group, although African American parents are no more likely to abuse or neglect their children. And I did not know that several studies over the course of several decades have determined that "race is the most consistent factor contributing to the decision to remove children and place them in foster care." I knew only that the stories I saw unfolding in front of me were disturbing enough to suggest the possibility that black children were now routinely confiscated by the government for the same reasons that black men and women were once sterilized by the government. But that was not something I could report.

Shortly after her fingerprints were taken, Ms. Johnson was told by a social worker that because her felony was more than ten years old, it would not affect her ability to take custody of her grandchildren. Inspectors came to her apartment, and she was told that it would be suitable for the children on a temporary basis but that she would eventually have to move.

So Ms. Johnson was preparing for her grandchildren to move in with her, buying clothes and shoes and bed linens for them, when she was informed by a second social worker that not ten but twelve years must have passed after her conviction before she could have the children. It had been, at that time, about eleven and a half years since her conviction. When she wrote CPS to find out whether the time period was ten years or twelve, she received a letter from a third social worker informing her that it was twenty years.

I sifted through all these letters, called social workers who would not talk to me or would not call me back, made time lines, and read Ms. Johnson's foster-care manual. A tradition of caring for children within kinship networks, the manual informed me, is an integral part of African American culture. After being redirected many times, eventually to the licensing department at CPS, I learned that generally an individual is eligible to serve as a foster parent if ten years have passed after a felony conviction. But, I was told, these decisions are made on a "case-by-case basis."

Meanwhile, Ms. Johnson went to court hearings, met with social workers, completed the tasks outlined by CPS in the Family Unity Meeting agreement, and, once a week, took the bus to McDonald's for a one-hour visit with her grandchildren. Often the foster parents were late in bringing the children, or didn't make it at all, so Ms. Johnson would wait for an hour and then return home to leave a message on the answering machine of the social worker. At one point, the children were moved to a new foster home, and Ms. Johnson couldn't find out where they were. They were not brought to McDonald's, and CPS didn't return her calls.

Ms. Johnson was a letter writer. She wrote letters to the director of CPS about not knowing where her grandchildren were, she wrote letters to social workers about her rights as a family member, which she had researched, and, when Ms. Johnson realized that her case was turning on an eleven-and-a-half-year-old conviction, she wrote to the judge who had served her with probation. She then discovered that she was eligible to have her conviction expunged, and six months after her grandchildren had been placed in foster care, a judge ordered her record cleared.

Soon after her record was cleared, Ms. Johnson's grandchildren were moved into a concurrent-planning home, meaning a home with a family who wanted to adopt the children. Ms. Johnson wrote a letter to CPS complaining about this, explaining that she had been working toward taking custody of the children for quite some time. She was then told that her housing was inadequate. If she could find a new place to live and move before the next hearing date, she could have the children. This was in mid-September—the next hearing was set for October 29.

Ms. Johnson had taken the parenting classes mandated by CPS, and she had taken workshops on teamwork, self-esteem, and understanding depression in children. She had completed her CPR certification, and she had, as she would point out in her letters, "the certificates to prove it." But she didn't have the children.

The editor of the *Voice* did not give me a word limit for my story about Ms. Johnson, but nevertheless there were things I did not report. I did not report, for example, that she had shown me a picture of her light-skinned grandchildren. I did not report that she thought the social workers were keeping the children from her because they looked white and could be placed with a white family who wanted to adopt white children. And I did not report that when I asked Ms. Johnson if she had any idea why CPS wouldn't let her take custody of her grandchildren, she said, "Because I'm too black."

"We have a gag order," the editor of the *Voice* informed me, with a mixture of anger and excitement, a few days after my article ran on the front page. According to Ms. Johnson, the judge assigned to her case had ordered her not to talk to any more reporters and had warned her that talking to the newspaper was a "breach of contract" and that he could sentence her to six months in jail if he wanted to. At the time, it didn't occur to me to wonder if that was true. It didn't occur to me to ask exactly what contract was being breached, and I suspect now that it didn't occur to Ms. Johnson either.

I'm not sure exactly at what point I lost heart, at what point I knew for sure that I could not be a reporter, but I quit my job not very long after my last interview with Ms. Johnson. For a time after I left the *Voice and Viewpoint,* the news in the *New York Times* no longer read like news to me. It read like someone else's fantasy. And it would be years, it would be until after the levees broke in New Orleans, before I would read anything in the national news that bore a resemblance to the news as it was collected in the *Voice and Viewpoint.*

In the days after the levees broke, the mayor was cussing on the radio and Kanye West was saying, "George Bush doesn't care about black people." Thousands of people were waiting in the Superdome for two days and then four and then six. It was the ten years that became twelve that became twenty for Ms. Johnson. And in New Orleans reporters from all over the country seemed genuinely horrified. They'd never covered this beat. "This doesn't seem like America," they kept saying. "This just doesn't seem possible in America."

Letter to Mexico

I am sending you a photocopy of a passage from the book *Shame and Its Sisters*. This photocopy was sent to me not long after I returned from Mexico, by the man who was my traveling companion there. It begins, "If I wish to touch you but do not wish to be touched, I may feel ashamed."

If you were to ask me now, "Why did you go to Mexico?" I would not be able to answer you honestly. I might say that I went to learn a language I have been trying to learn for a decade and still cannot speak.

Shame and Its Sisters continues, "If I wish to look at you but you do not wish me to, I may feel ashamed. . . . If I wish to look at you and at the same time wish that you look at me, I can be shamed. If I wish to be close to you but you move away, I am ashamed."

As we drove across the border I saw a long line of people waiting to go to work in San Diego, their bicycles locked on the fence near customs. In the months before leaving for Mexico, I took a Spanish class at San Diego Community College taught by a woman who commuted from Tijuana. Sometimes, she told us in class, it took her more than two hours to get across the border. That Spanish class is the only course I have ever failed.

Once across the border, there was a wall of corrugated metal that we drove along, and razor wire, and a ditch, and a lone man carrying a plastic bag in the sun, and a sudden change in the surface of the landscape, which I did not anticipate, because San Diego and Tijuana are closer than sisters, almost two halves of the same city. But San Diego is green along the highways, and Tijuana is not. In San Diego, dusk brings the rhythmic sound of sprinklers, but here it does not.

The Colorado River is split down its deepest channel by the border. So much water is drawn off by both countries that the river rarely reaches the ocean anymore. Every day, a good part of Mexico's share of that water is used to cool the turbines at two new power plants in Mexicali. The plants are owned by American companies, and most of the power they generate is sold to California and Arizona. These power plants and two thousand maquiladoras, American-owned factories along the border, are the fruits of the North American Free Trade Agreement, which has been in effect for more than a decade. The ten-year reports on NAFTA reveal that Mexico, like the United States, now has a small number of billionaires. And the real wages for everyone else have fallen. One of the promises of NAFTA was that it would make Mexico more like the

United States. And it did—in that it widened the gap between the richest people in Mexico and the poorest.

When we stopped, after driving south for an hour, in a very small town with one cantina, which was also a motel, I asked a woman standing by the bar, *"Por favor, necesitamos un cuarto para esta noche."* It was a sentence I had repeated over and over to myself in the car until I could say it somewhat casually. The woman said, "Hold on honey," and pulled me by the arm up to the bartender, saying, "Ramón, this little girl doesn't speak English."

In La Salina that evening all the Americans were having their weekly potluck at the cantina. I would discover that beyond the guarded gate next to the cantina, the town of La Salina was inhabited almost exclusively by Americans. Ramón, the bartender, and Gustavo, the waiter, spoke English, and no one else, as far as I could tell, spoke Spanish. That night, while firecrackers popped outside on the beach and strains of "La Bamba" and "Achy Breaky Heart" pounded through the floor of my room, I realized that I could never leave my country. I could check out any time I liked, as the song goes, but I could never leave.

I woke up to the sound of a man throwing rocks at the streetlight that lighted the patio behind the cantina at night. It was the same streetlight that this man had boasted was illegally wired so that it ran off power stolen from Mexico. The Americans were going to have a bonfire, and they wanted the patio to be dark. After one of his rocks hit something beyond the wall, making a cracking sound, the man dropped the rocks and slunk away like a naughty boy.

When I first arrived in La Salina, I had the illusion that the Americans there were outlaws. I thought that I had stumbled upon a community of people who were wanted for serious crimes in the United States. I would later realize exactly how fanciful this idea was, and how ignorant of economics, but for a time this was how I would interpret the nightly fireworks and the stolen electricity and the fight in the bar and my sense that I was among cowboy impersonators and gold prospectors. It now seems unlikely to me that the Americans in La Salina were guilty of anything more than ordinary poverty and a distinctly American desire to live the good life. But they were indeed, in the tradition of the old West, prospectors.

Two men, in particular, were often talking loudly out on the patio about what they could build and what they could sell and what it would cost and what they would make. One of them, I gathered, owned the cantina, and the other seemed to have some interest in it. Their calculations were like NAFTA negotiations on a small scale, in that they were always banking on getting the cheapest possible materials and paying as little as possible for labor. But NAFTA wasn't designed to benefit small operations, and if these guys weren't rich already, they probably weren't going to be, no matter whom they cheated.

In Spanish, the word for "border" is *frontera*—sounding like the English word "frontier," which can mean "the border between two countries." Or, according to my dictionary, "the extreme limit of understanding."

In the cantina one evening, a Mexican man with a guitar was singing. I heard his voice through the floor of my room, and when

I came down for dinner we talked a bit about his Hollywood ambitions. Later, he would suggest that I write the story of his life, but I would never see him again. *"Cucurrucucu,"* he sang, *"paloma."* The song was about a dove who cries for her lost lover. *"Cucurrucucu,"* he sang, *"cucurrucucu, cucurrucucu, paloma, ya no llores."* I was slightly drunk on my second margarita and the song was bringing tears to my eyes when a gringo at the bar interrupted by shouting, "Hey, who wrote that?" The song was a folk song with no known author, but the man persisted, "Who wrote that?"

"A couple of pigeons," the singer said finally, still looking at his guitar, not the gringo.

I felt sick with hatred then for my own people. If you had asked me then why I hated them, I might have said that I hated them for being so loud and for being so drunk. But now I believe I hated them for suddenly being my people, not just other people. In the United States, it is very easy for me to forget that the people around me are my people. It is easy, with all our divisions, to think of myself as an outsider in my own country. I have been taught, and I have learned well, I realize now, to think of myself as distinctly different from other white folks—more educated, more articulate, less crude. But in Mexico these distinctions became as meaningless to me as they should have always been.

A few months before I left for Mexico, after having four teeth pulled in San Diego—which cost me my entire savings, because I had no dental insurance—I noticed, in the Laundromat that was a block from my apartment, a gum-ball machine that vended "hillbilly teeth." These were a complete set of rotted, crooked, blackened, partially missing teeth that you could put over your own, presumably healthier teeth as a joke. I watched a little black boy buy some hillbilly teeth for a quarter and walk away with a parody of the problems of rural whites—a parody of loss and decay. In that moment I felt for my people.

Now, remembering that moment, I am reminded of James Baldwin in France. "His past," Baldwin wrote of the black American expatriate, "he now realizes, has not been simply a series of ropes and bonfires and humiliations, but something vastly more complex, which, as he thinks painfully, 'It was much worse than that,' was also, he irrationally feels, something much better."

My past, I discovered in Mexico, was both simpler and more complicated than I had ever thought it to be. I had, very simply, enjoyed great privilege in life, and great opportunity. But it was much worse than that. I began to recognize at whose price I had enjoyed a comfortable life. This is not to say that I immediately understood the intricacies of international trade agreements—it is only to say that I felt a nameless, crushing remorse.

In La Salina, I sat at the bar with Americans whom I disdained for their greed and ignorance. But I was there for the same reason they were. Because in La Salina I could afford to stay on the beach for the money I made as a receptionist in San Diego.

"Why La Salina Del Mar?" asked an ad for lots and houses and condos that would soon be built on the hill next to La Salina.

- The closest reasonably priced lots in Mexico
- Building costs below current U.S. rates
- Access by modern dual highway
- Retirement living within everyone's reach

Retirement living within everyone's reach. Affordable ocean-front. Freedom and fireworks for all. This is what Mexico had to offer us. And we were happy to take it.

The beach in La Salina was a glorious beach. It smelled like gasoline and horse dung, and the Americans there were all fat and ravaged by sun and alcohol and cigarettes. Tattered blonds in T-shirts carried drinks to paunchy old men on the patio. There were dirty white towels, ants in the carpet, rust in the sink, ATVs roaring across the beach, dogs chasing the ATVs, and two giant, fanlike flying machines that buzzed back and forth above the surf all day. Horses strolled by as I stood on the balcony watching, girls on motorcycles tossed up sand, and some guys at the top of the beach hit golf balls and hooted.

During my time in Mexico, I would return to La Salina every weekend. And I would return with relief. I would swim in the ocean there, drink at the bar, read in my room, and stand on the balcony, watching the surf and a Jeep full of gringos that was about to topple into the surf. On an average day, the song "Hotel California" played about once an hour in the cantina at La Salina. I don't know who decided this, but old Ramón, who controlled what stations played silently on the TVs, certainly might have been responsible. He seemed nearly as weary as that song began to sound to me. In my most vivid memory of La Salina, I am standing in the shade of the cantina, on the patio outside the bar, feeling remorse, looking at the back of my companion's reddening neck where he sits reading in the sun with a gallon of water next to him, and the ocean far ahead of him, and I hear, in between the faint sounds of pool balls from inside, "They're livin' it up at the Hotel California. . . ."

"Hotel California" was a hit song the year I was born. It was playing on all the radios, and its lyrics now are the only photograph I have of the moment I was born into. "Mirrors on the ceiling," Don Henley sings, "the pink champagne on ice. And she said, 'We are all just prisoners here of our own device.' And in the master's chambers they gathered for the feast. They stab it with their steely knives but they just can't kill the beast."

Perhaps the story of Mexican immigrants coming to America for a better life has been told so many times that it has obscured the reality of American expatriates fleeing to Mexico for the life they have been promised but not delivered. And perhaps this is why, in the cantina in La Salina, the song "Hotel California" was so haunting to me. As I grew used to hearing it, it took on the kind of raw, heartbreaking humor that I found in the black boy buying hillbilly teeth from a gum-ball machine in the San Diego Laundromat. It was the same humor I found in the small statues of skeletons dressed as doctors that were sold in the tourist district of Ensenada. I bought one of these skeleton doctors for my father, a doctor, but later found it very difficult to explain to him why.

I stayed in the cantina at La Salina on weekends, but during the week, while I was taking Spanish classes in Ensenada, I stayed in the home of a Mexican family. The father was a doctor, like my father, and the mother taught at the Spanish school where I took classes. Their daughter had just returned from a semester abroad in Kansas, and their son led tours for Americans over where the cruise ships docked. The house they lived in was surrounded by a high cement wall, and the wall was topped with broken glass. If I had grown up in Mexico, I realized, I too would have grown up behind a wall. At meals, the mother reminded me how to say "napkin" and we talked of very little else because I lacked the words I needed to say anything meaningful. My companion initiated one halting conversation about the Zapatistas, which ended in us all staring at the television, where *Terminator* was playing with Spanish subtitles. One evening, the father forgot his keys and stood on the street, where he could just barely see me reading by the window above the wall, and he yelled for an hour before I realized that it was him yelling and that he was saying, in Spanish, "Child! Child! Open the door! Let me in!"

That phrase and my inability to hear it echo now through my memory of Mexico, along with the sounds of roosters and birds and the endless honks of the water truck as it made its morning rounds. In Ensenada, the horn of the water truck makes the high A of a violin tuning before a concert, giving the mornings there the sound of the moments before some grand concert of dogs and cars and metal on concrete. Outside my window, beyond the wall topped with broken glass, kids played in the dried-up canal, throwing rocks or riding bikes without seats down a sandy bank.

Walking the streets of Ensenada felt to me like walking along the edge of the ocean. I was confined to the shore there, even when I was not in the tourist district, where the cruise ships unloaded and middle-aged Americans periodically swarmed the bars and souvenir stands then receded like a tide. I was confined to the shore even in the alleys, even in the bodegas, even in the house where I slept. At first, I smiled eagerly and hopefully at everyone who looked at me on the street in Ensenada. Soon, when I was not looking at the ground, I looked at everyone the same way they looked at me, with a wary expressionlessness.

I would walk to school in the dust, on the broken sidewalks, through the stares, past the skinny dogs that stood up and followed me with their eyes before they lay back down. I would pass the truck piled high with bunches of clean radishes, where I would buy a *torta* for lunch and then wash my hands with the juice of a lime. I would pass shacks made of corrugated metal and lines of laundry and a row of pickle jars full of peaches and strawberries and mangos waiting to be poured over ice. I would read signs, and I would understand some of what I heard, but not all of it. Not nearly all of it.

Signs for candidates in the local elections were plastered all over the telephone poles, but I knew even less about local politics than I knew about national politics. I did not know then that NAFTA had in effect eroded many of the rights and protections provided by the Mexican constitution. I did not know that breaking strikes had become a common practice under

NAFTA, even after the federal court ruled in 1999 that strikes were legal. I did not know, really, anything.

One afternoon in Ensenada, I stopped in a *farmacia,* where I picked up a Popsicle and some aspirin. The store was not in the tourist district, and it was empty in the afternoon heat. The girl at the register stood looking out the window with her shoulder to me, where I stood waiting at the counter. She was very still, and her long hair fluttered up in an arc every time the rotating fan turned in her direction. She would not look at me, even when I murmured, "Cuanto cuesta?" She would not look at me and would not say anything. Finally, I put down a bill, and she slapped down change, still not turning to face me. I left with tears in my eyes, holding, pathetically, a melting Popsicle.

The fact that I was hated in Baja California was not lost on me for a moment. At times, I cherished the delusion that I could blame the fact that I was hated on the loud and rowdy Americans who flooded the restaurants and bars in the tourist district with an alarming sense of ownership. But now I understand that they were just a way for me to think about American excesses. Most of the Americans in the bars were as damaged by those excesses as Mexico was.

In my mornings and afternoons of walking, I had plenty of time to think about being hated, and I often, after thinking on it for a while, concluded that I deserved to be hated. At times, I was as sure of this as I was sure I deserved the F that I had received in my Spanish class in San Diego, but I still did not understand exactly how personally implicated I should feel. I knew that my body and my presence there meant something, spoke something to everyone who saw me, but I did not know what. And I still do not know, but I suspect it was something about everything America was stealing from Mexico.

I was relieved of the sensation of being hated only when I went to La Salina for the weekends, where I could indulge in hating other Americans. Even after four weekends I could not admit that the hatred I felt for the Americans in the cantina at La Salina was the hatred I felt for myself—a punishment for being so ignorant of the world outside my country and for eating all the pomegranate seeds I had ever been offered. In all my time in La Salina, I managed never to exchange more than a few words with another American. I did not ask anyone how they got there, or why they lived there, or what they had left behind. I tried, for the most part, to talk only to Mexicans. And for the most part I failed.

In school in Ensenada I learned the words for many different kinds of food and some parts of the body. I did not learn how to say, "The excesses of my country are paid for by your country." But I learned to say, "I have a stomachache." And in one of my final lessons, I learned the construction *me da vergüenza*. Literally, "it gives me shame."

I would, while I was in Mexico, read over and over a letter that had been written to me by a woman I worked with in San Diego. For some time in San Diego after I quit my job as a reporter I worked only on my own writing. But after my teeth were pulled, I temped as a receptionist at a chemical factory in Chula Vista. I now understand, having learned a few things about NAFTA, why this factory was so close to the border and why they wanted a receptionist who could speak Spanish. But at the time I was happy to be entirely unaware of nearly everything that went on in the chemical factory. I spent my days there forwarding calls and printing a several-thousand-page document that needed to be printed one page at a time, for reasons I did not care to understand. From where I sat, I could see the sign that I drove past every morning on my way in to work:

WARNING

Beyond this point are chemicals known
to the state of California to be hazardous. . . .

I was supposed to be a bilingual receptionist, able to handle calls in both Spanish and English. Often, when I needed to speak more than a few words of Spanish on the phone I would panic and ask for help from Rosa, who worked across the office. In turn, Rosa would ask me to correct her English on memos and in letters. We spoke very haltingly in each other's languages of how difficult it is to learn a new language. I told her that I was going to go to Mexico so that I could learn faster. She told me she was sure that would help. On the day I left the factory, Rosa ran out into the parking lot as I was getting into my car and handed me a letter, then ran back inside.

Dear Friend,

This is your last day working with our Company and
I just want to tell you thank you for every thing, thank
you for your help and Keep Smiling. You know what?
Usually in this days the people don't pay attention to

the small details but Keep Smiling no matter what happen and my best wishes for you, you are young and have a long live in front of you, you are very smart and I'm sure you can be true to all your goals, try to learn as more you can from the places and from the people that you meat. And don't forget that God have a special plans for you.

Sincerely,
Rosa

P.D.T. You know what? When I came to this country I started working in a Restaurant washing Dishes, in a factory the worst work in all my life, Construction drywall with men, dirty clothes hard job, but you know what in my country I study Human resources in the University and all the times the only think that make my stand up is an ilution that one day every thing go better for me. And now this is not an excellent job but I'm happy.

I tried, several times, to answer this letter in Spanish. I sat and made two or three words with the help of my dictionary. "Querida Rosa," I always began. In the end, I never answered Rosa's letter, and I never heard from her again.

We joined the line, eventually, of cars leaving Mexico. The line was miles long, and the cars were mostly minivans and Jeeps and SUVs with California plates. Our enormous motorcade crawled past a man standing by the side of the road, holding up a giant plaster cast of *The Last Supper*. I did not understand, at first, that *The Last Supper* was for sale. I saw the gesture as some kind of beautiful protest.

At the next intersection, men with buckets washed windows, and I watched one man cross himself quickly after being paid with change. The road had become six lanes wide, all stopped with traffic. An Indian woman with long braids walked between the cars, selling peanuts, a baby bound to her body. All the people around the cars now were Indians, and they seemed to be streaming onto the highway directly from their fields of corn that no longer existed, still sun baked and dusty. A little girl ran between the cars, selling cigarettes, and a very small boy stood motionless between two lanes of traffic, holding out a plastic cup, vacant-faced as cars streamed around him.

On New Year's Day in 1994, the same day NAFTA was implemented, there was an uprising of Indian peasants in Chiapas. NAFTA, the Zapatista army declared, was a "death sentence" for the indigenous people of Mexico. While Clinton was promising that NAFTA would "lift all boats," the Zapatistas warned that NAFTA would bring falling prices for corn, falling wages for workers, and the loss of land to foreign investors. That is exactly what happened. Because Iowa corn imported into Mexico is heavily subsidized by the United States government, the price of corn in Mexico fell by half during the first ten years of NAFTA. More than a million farmers were displaced from their land and forced to migrate to the cities or the United States, where they became day laborers, picking U.S. crops.

Next to our car, all along the side of the road, men sold rugs printed with American flags and painted plaster statues of Woodstock, Spider-Man, and Betty Boop. In the traffic, men and women and children sold fried dough, crucifixes, Doritos, and Fritos. Little girls with braids and no front teeth raised their eyebrows and held out cups when our eyes met.

I watched all this and I felt pure despair. I put change in the cups and I felt despair.

It was getting dark and it began to rain as we approached the border. Two little girls near our car were singing. One absently fixed her sandal with her hand while she sang. She seemed to be in good spirits, despite the sudden cold. The heat was on in our car and the windows were fogging. Ahead of us, a man unrolled his window to give the girl two quarters. Without missing a beat, still stamping time with one foot, she handed one quarter to the girl next to her. Their voices rose above the sound of hundreds of motors idling and mingled with the fumes.

Babylon

The hanging gardens were built for a homesick wife. Amytis of the Medes found the flat, dry land of Babylon depressing, and so her gardens were planted on terraces to look like hillsides.

"The air in California," my cousin once told me in New York, "smells like flowers." At the time, I took this as nostalgia for her home, but when I moved to California I found that it was true, especially in Oakland, where bougainvillea climbed telephone poles and huge hibiscus flowers poured out over the front yards of all the little houses.

The people of Babylon did not grow figs or grapes or olives, wrote Herodotus, but the land of Assyria was so rich that the fields of grain produced two hundred–fold or even three hundred–fold. He is thought to have exaggerated.

My first disappointment in California was the park. At the end of the summer it was a wasteland of brittle shrubbery. But the winter rains would make the park green, and I would learn that it was full of gardens.

Their exile in Babylon, their captivity, was, for the Jews, both a punishment and a promise. It was through this exile that God would deliver his people.

Palm trees were all I saw as my plane landed in California, and palm trees were all I could see there for a long time. The palm trees were how I knew I was a long way from home.

There was a garden in the park called the Desert Garden, where African bottle trees and pencil trees and strange succulents grew. At midday this garden was hot and still, the yellow dirt paths were pounded hard, and almost all the plants were scarred from graffiti. There were messages etched into the leaves of the agaves and up the trunks of the saguaros, between the spines. Most were declarations of love: "Edgar R Te Amo Rosa," "Sang Love Thuy," "Victoria y Bernardo," "Lilia + Maryus," "Isidro y Blanca ♥ nuestro hija Leslie."

Plants deal with their wounds differently than we do. A cut on a plant will never heal, it will simply be sealed off or, at best, grown over. On one of our first days in California, my sister picked up the bright red fruit of a cactus from the ground and its tiny spines were in her fingers, swelling, for days.

"By their fruits ye shall know them," Matthew tells us. "Do men gather grapes of thorns, or figs of thistles?"

My sister and I drove out into the desert, only to discover that it was not, as I had imagined, empty. It was full of ocotillos and saguaros and crucifixion thorns.

I came to the fantasy of California early, twenty years before I moved there, because it was the place where my cousins lived. In third grade I wrote to the Oakland Chamber of Commerce and received, in the mail, a map of the city. This was in the eighties, when the crack houses of Oakland were still crack houses, not high-rent apartments. I pored over the map of Oakland, although the lines of it meant nothing to me then.

Oakland was advertised as a "garden city" by its postwar boosters. "Workmen," read one advertisement, "find happiness in their garden-set homes. . . . Their children are healthy in the mild, equable climate." The factories wanted workers who would not leave looking for something better.

But Americans always leave. We are a migrant people, a people of diasporas and exiles.

The two great migrations of the twentieth century, the migrations that made the landscape I was born into, were the migration of blacks to the cities and the migration of whites to the suburbs.

In the postwar decades, industry migrated too. The General Motors and Ford and Chevy plants left Oakland for the suburbs, and New York's textile district emptied.

The metaphor of Babylon, already employed by preachers and Rastafarians, entered, in the 1960s, the vocabulary of black politics. Babylon could stand for any city—for New York, for Oakland, for California, for the United States—for capitalism, for imperialism, or simply for excess. "It was often an elusive metaphor," Robert Self writes, "but it captured the profound cynicism engendered by decades of liberal failure as well as the remarkably optimistic belief in rebirth, in beginning again."

The fall of the city of Babylon was also the end of that particular captivity for the Jews. A reminder that there is always some promise in destruction.

Certain desert succulents can be forced to bloom by withholding water. And other plants can be forced to bloom with cold, or with cutting.

"For the Panthers and other black radicals," Robert Self writes, "the industrial garden of midcentury had become Babylon—a false city that had to be remade to stave off collapse."

By the seventies, landlords in New York City were abandoning their buildings. Squatters were taking over vacant tenements on the Lower East Side—patching roofs, rewiring electricity, building open fires, carrying buckets of water from fire hydrants, clearing the bricks and tires off empty lots to grow vegetables. On some blocks, they simply threw Christmas-tree ornaments full of wildflower seeds over the chain-link fences to break on the rubble. Seed bombs, they called these. And they called themselves homesteaders.

Meanwhile, exurbs. Penturbs. Boomburbs. Technoburbs. Sprinkler cities.

To flee within your own nation is to create a kind of captivity for yourself. A self-imposed exile. And so, the despair of the suburbs.

But to call it flight is to acknowledge only the fear and to ignore the other motivations, particularly the government subsidies— the highways, the mortgages, the tax breaks, the American dream.

I long, even now, to live in a place where I can have my own garden.

Because it is so sheltered by tall buildings, and so warmed by the "urban heat island effect," the climate of New York City is particularly suited to gardens of exile. The callaloo of Jamaica grows there, and the okra of Georgia, the peach tree of South Carolina and the tropical hibiscus.

Nonnative plants are sometimes called "invaders." Or, if we like them, "exotics." The apple tree, for one, is an exotic.

"The American traders and trappers who began settling in California as early as 1826 were leaving their country for a remote Mexican province, Alta California," writes Joan Didion. "Many became naturalized Mexican citizens. Many married into Mexican and Spanish families. A fair number received grants of land from the Mexican authorities." But when the

American immigrants rebelled against the Mexican government, most of them had been in California for less than a year.

Palm trees are not native to California. They come from Mexico, from Brazil, from Australia, from Costa Rica, from China, from Africa, from India, from Cuba—from, it seems, everywhere in the world except California.

Americans began their acquisition of Mexico by simply moving there. Even after the Mexican government prohibited American immigration to Texas, Americans continued to cross the border illegally. Stephen Austin, the "Father of Texas," urged Americans to come to Mexico, "passports or no passports."

After half of Mexico was claimed by the United States in 1848, thousands of Mexicans found themselves immigrants without ever having moved. In California, they outnumbered Americans by ten to one. They were made citizens of the United States, but they would, in the decades following the Treaty of Guadalupe Hidalgo, lose most of their land to drought, squatters, taxes, and American courts.

Now, some Americans fear a *reconquista* of the Southwest.

The iconic palms that line the streets and boulevards of Southern California are dying of age and disease. They were planted when the cities were young, and the cities are no longer young.

Oakland was once a woodland of oaks. It was named *Encinal,* "oak land," by the Spanish rancher who owned it before the gold rush.

In Los Angeles, the rows of dying palms along the boulevards may soon be replaced by oaks.

Almost two million more people left California in the 1990s than came there from the rest of the country. They went, mostly, to the mountain states, to Colorado, Montana, Idaho. "Lifestyle migrants," they were called. A native Californian who left for Idaho told *USA Today,* "I was getting tired of traffic, graffiti, dirty air."

But graffiti, we all know, is not a reason to leave the place where you were born.

"A lot of people coming in from California," observed a professor at the University of Montana, "are coming in for 'urban dread' reasons."

In the nineties, after New York had resisted collapse and the land on the Lower East Side became valuable again, the city began to bulldoze gardens on empty lots to make way for new buildings. By then, the gardens had stone paths and goldfish ponds and grape trellises and roses.

Graffiti is one way to claim a place you do not own. And so is planting a garden. Because we are all forever in exile, or so the story goes, from the original garden.

Date palms belong to the genus *Phoenix,* and in California they rise from the ashes of conquest. *Phoenix canariensis* is the Canary Island date palm, brought by the Franciscan priest who founded the mission that became San Diego, and *Phoenix roebelenii* is the pygmy date palm, and *Phoenix dactylifera* is the true date palm.

Some of the community gardens of lower Manhattan had already been razed when I moved to New York, but there was still a hanging garden in the old meatpacking district—the elevated train tracks, no longer in use, had grown tall weeds and wildflowers.

"The daughter of Babylon," Jeremiah tells us, "is like a threshing-floor, it is time to thresh her: yet a little while, and the time of her harvest shall come."

My cousin and I stood together once, by the Long Island Railroad tracks, under a sign that read "Babylon." As I looked down the long gray tracks netted with electric lines, my cousin looked up at the sign and said, "Well, they call it what it is out here."

My grandmother keeps a garden on the graves of her parents, who came all the way from Poland to die in New York. Her most precious plants grow there, in the most permanent place she knows. She gave me some lilies of the valley from that garden, and I planted them in the shade of my father's house in the suburbs not long before he moved away and I left for California.

"They tended to accommodate any means in pursuit of an uncertain end," Joan Didion writes of the pioneer women in her family, the women who went West. "They tended to avoid dwelling on just what that end might imply. When they could not think what else to do they moved another thousand miles, set out another garden: beans and squash and sweet peas from seeds carried from the last place. The past could be jettisoned, children buried and parents left behind, but seeds got carried."

I spent my first summer in New York City walking through the gardens of Far Rockaway, gardens that covered entire blocks forgotten by the city. They had paths of old carpet between rows of sunflowers. I walked through gardens in Harlem and the Bronx full of beads and candles and statues of the Virgin Mary enshrined in little wooden *casitas*. One man told me that he had everything he needed to survive Y2K in his garden.

I heard a rumor in California, which I never had occasion to test, that if you were stranded out in the desert, you could cut off the top of a barrel cactus and find a reservoir of fresh water within.

Next to the highway running through the desert outside San Diego, there were gallon jugs of water buried for those trying to make their way into the country on foot. A priest from LA had brought the jugs of water to the desert in his minivan and buried them with the help of volunteers. The water was marked with blue flags bleached by the sun, and some jugs were buried where bodies had been found. That this water had been brought all the way out there and was truly under those blue flags seemed as impossible to me as the telephone poles that persisted through the heart of the desert.

The hanging gardens of Babylon may never have existed. Herodotus never mentions them, and they are absent from the Babylonian records. But the other defining feature of the city, its immense walls, described by Herodotus as 80 feet thick and 320 feet high, were real enough to crumble with time.

The Midwest

Back to Buxton

Each of us has certain clichés, I suspect, to which we are particularly vulnerable, certain songs we are compelled to play over and over again, certain words that undo us with their simple syllables. For years now I have been unable to think clearly if the lyrics of "Sweet Home Alabama" are within my hearing, or "Take Me Home, Country Roads," or even "Long Walk Home."

Not long after I began college, when it was dawning on me that, having left my family, I would never again feel as essential, as integral, as I had once felt among them, a friend of mine said, "You know, you can never go home." Because I did not yet recognize that phrase as a cliché, the truth of it rang through me like a gong.

And that was even before I really, truly left home—before I moved from the familiar landscape of rural Massachusetts to New York City, and then to San Diego, and then to Iowa City. Iowa City, where I would eventually find myself sitting alone in a small, windowless room in a big university library, crying while I watched, for the second time, the videotape of an Iowa Public Television documentary titled *You Can't Go Back to Buxton*.

Buxton, Iowa, is now just a stack of bricks and a small flock of gravestones in a farmer's field, but was once an unincorporated mining camp of five thousand, an integrated town with a majority-black population in the mostly white state of Iowa during the Jim Crow era. Buxton was built in 1900, and it was a ghost town by 1920, but it continues on in books and songs and folklore and public-television documentaries as a myth and a specter and, as I came to see it, a kind of promise. But before I understood Buxton's significance in that way, I understood it as I did when I was sitting in the library among boxes of documents waiting to be archived, leaning toward the small television where old folks in faded living rooms spoke of Buxton in that deeply wistful way that is reserved only for the place you came from.

I came, at one time, from a place by a river, where we lived under the flight path of an airport and I could see the rivets on the bottoms of the passenger jets as they passed overhead. It was a place of unmown fields and sand pits and backwaters where I rode my bike with boys whose houses were flooded by the rising river every spring.

Now, the road through that place has widened by several lanes and is lined with Kmarts and Wal-Marts and a mall called Latham Farms, which sits on land where there were once, in my childhood, actual farms. The airport has sheared off the tops of trees for greater visibility, the next-door neighbor who used to give me books about Sodom and Gomorrah has died, both of my parents have moved away, and I will never live there again.

On the evening of my first day in Iowa, in a humid darkness full of the purring of cicadas, I finally went down to the river, where I had been waiting to go all day, ever since I first saw the water from the car as I drove into town that afternoon. When I stepped onto the bridge over the Iowa River and stood looking out across the water, I knew I was home. I was wrong about that, as it turns out. And I know now that my certainty was based on a series of troubling misconceptions, but it would be years before I would lose the comfort that certainty gave me. At that moment the air over the river smelled thick and slightly fishy and sweet with grass and leaves, like all the Augusts of my childhood. And as I looked down into the water, where some tremendously huge carp were swimming against the current, I thanked God for bringing me home.

Buxton was a company town, owned and operated by Consolidated Coal. Located an equal distance from three mines, on a gently sloping hill, Buxton was more carefully planned than most coal camps, which were often roughly built, poorly drained temporary barracks next to the coal tipples. The houses Consolidated built for its workers were bigger than those in most coal camps, and they were set far enough apart to allow for gardens. The miners in Buxton were not required to buy their goods from the company store and thus not required to go into debt to the company. Buxton had two roller-skating rinks, a swimming pool, and a YMCA sponsored by Consolidated Coal. Buxton was larger than most coal camps, and it would thrive for twice as long, but, like any other camp, it would last only as long as the mines. When the town began to empty after a fire and the collapse of one mine, it emptied very rapidly, so that by 1919 there were only about four hundred people left in Buxton.

Initially, the population of Buxton was just over half black, and it would eventually drop to just under half black. Some of the black miners in Buxton may have originally been recruited by Consolidated to break a strike in an all-white mine nearby. When that mine shut, most of the miners there, many of them black, were relocated to Buxton. It was common, during that period, for companies to pit one racial group against another— sugarcane planters in Hawaii hired Portuguese workers to break the strikes of Japanese workers, the owner of a shoe factory in Massachusetts broke a strike of Irish workers by hiring Chinese immigrants, and the Central Pacific Railroad in California considered bringing ten thousand blacks across the country to break a strike of Chinese workers. Some historians have suggested that we have early capitalism to thank for the traditional animosity in this country between racial groups who vied for jobs. But that animosity didn't take in Buxton. The management of the mine was actively recruiting black workers from the South until at least 1910, but those workers were not breaking strikes in Buxton or working for lower wages than the white workers. And they were not, for the most part, locked out of the most desirable or the most lucrative jobs in the mines. Both black and white miners in Buxton belonged to the United Mine Workers, a union that demanded equal pay for equal work.

The editor of the *Iowa State Bystander,* an African American newspaper, described Buxton as "the colored man's mecca of Iowa" and the "Negro Athens of the Northwest." Buxton had integrated schools and an integrated baseball team, the Buxton Wonders. Both blacks and whites operated independent businesses in town. There was a black dentist, a black tailor, a black midwife, black newspaper publishers, black doctors, black pharmacists, black lawyers, black undertakers, a black postmaster, a black justice of the peace, black constables, black teachers and principals, and black members of the school board.

In Buxton, Dorothy Collier's family had a green plush sofa and a new cookstove. Marjorie Brown's family had a carpet and a piano in the parlor. "In Buxton," Bessie Lewis said, "you didn't have to want for nothing." It was a prosperous place. But, more than that, it was a place that enjoyed unusually good race relations. And this is why former residents would describe it as "a kind of heaven." This is why they would continue to return for picnics forty years after Consolidated Coal had dismantled the last of the houses there. And this is why three scholars from Iowa State University would set out to study the town in the early 1980s, to determine if it had been as racially harmonious as it was rumored to have been. Their results were not the results one might expect from such a study. After interviewing seventy-five former residents, black and white, after analyzing payroll records and census records and company records, after reading decades of local-newspaper accounts, after looking for evidence of discrimination in housing and schooling, they determined that, yes, Buxton had been "a utopia."

I enjoyed, when I first arrived in Iowa City, a kind of giddy, blind happiness. By then I had moved often enough not to have the usual illusions about a clean slate or a fresh start or a new life. I knew that I could not escape myself. And the idea of beginning again, with no furniture and no friends, was exhausting. So my happiness then is hard to explain. I am tempted now to believe that entering the life one is meant to inhabit is a thrilling sensation and that is all. But I am haunted by the possibility that I was happy when I arrived in Iowa at least in part because of my misconception that I had come to a place where the people were like me.

At the time, I am sure I would have denied that race had anything to do with my sense of belonging, but I would not have denied that certain everyday actions, like walking to the grocery store, were more comfortable because I was not in a place where my race was noticed. A friend of mine once described reveling in the anonymity of Harlem after having grown up on Cape Cod, where his family was one of only a few black families. In Harlem, he told me, he was invisible for the first time in his life. And another friend of mine, a black woman, once described to me her experience of walking through a Wal-Mart in rural Iowa, where she was stared at until she could not bear the attention anymore. Her husband had suggested that she take off her glasses so that she could not see the stares, and that, she said, had helped.

There are plenty of things, I now know, that I value much more than invisibility. But at the time when I moved to Iowa City, I longed for it. I was tired of being seen, and, worse, of seeing myself be seen. I was tired of that odd caricature of myself that danced in front of me like a puppet as I walked through the streets of places where my race was noticed. In those places I saw, as I imagined everyone else did, my whiteness, dancing there, mocking me, daring me to try to understand it. And I tried. But by the time I arrived in Iowa I was frustrated by the effort, and ready to remove my glasses.

If invisibility was all I expected out of Iowa City, I would never have become disillusioned there. In the end I suffered not for lack of anonymity, but for lack of a community to which I belonged in some essential way. Iowa City was a town of writers, a town where the waitresses and the bartenders and the guys who changed the oil in my car were writers, and it was a town of scholars, a liberal town—a town, in other words, full of people like me. But belonging, I would learn there, is much more complicated than that.

It was in the late nineteenth century, Lewis Atherton writes, that people in the towns of the Middle West began to lose their sense of belonging to the larger communities in which they lived. And so began what he calls "the twentieth century cult of joining." In Buxton, a town of only five thousand, a town a fraction of the size of Iowa City, a town in which members of almost every family worked in some capacity for the mines, there were dozens of social clubs and secret societies. There was the

Odd Fellows lodge, the Masonic Order, the Benevolent and
Protective Order of the Elks, the True Reformers, the Ladies
Industrial Club, the Sweet Magnolia Club, the Fidelity Club,
the Mutual Benefit Literary Society, the Etude Music Club, the
Self-Culture Club....

I don't belong to any clubs and haven't since I was a child.
I don't go to church, I don't play any team sports, and I pay my
union dues without attending meetings. Not being a joiner, I
am forced to believe, even at this late date, one hundred years
after Buxton, in the larger community. And so I am forced to be
frustrated by the many forces that thwart communities. One
of those being, in college towns, the fact that the majority of
the population is transient and uninvested and somewhat displaced. And then, of course, there is the fact that college towns
are company towns, towns owned, more or less, by institutions, towns polluted by the same problems that plague those
institutions.

During my last year in Iowa City, the university released
a lengthy report written by the diversity action committee. It
was, to me, a troubling and contradictory document. It began
with a series of recommendations for recruiting more minority
students to the school, followed by some disturbing findings,
particularly that many minority students were not especially
happy at the university. "Once minority students arrive at the
University, many report feeling alienated and alone," the report
stated. "Some express frustration that the depictions of the diversity of the University community and Iowa City found on
the University's website and in its printed materials are misleading, and some students are shocked to find the minority

community—currently 2,678 students of a total student body of 29,642—so small and so dispersed."

The point at which I began to cry during the documentary about Buxton was the interview with Marjorie Brown, who moved from Buxton to the mostly white town of Cedar Rapids when she was twelve. "And then all at once, with no warning, I no longer existed. . . . The shock of my life was to go to Cedar Rapids and find out that I didn't exist. . . . I had to unlearn that Marjorie was an important part of a community."

This was not a comfortable invisibility—this was obscurity. This was, in her words, the loss of her self. And this is what goes unspoken in many of the stories of integration that are told now as stories of heroism and triumph. This is what I heard in the voice of a man on the radio who, when asked what it was like for him to move to an all-white suburb of Chicago in the sixties, explained that he had children, and that he could put them in better schools there. He wouldn't say, exactly, what it felt like, but he implied it was a sacrifice.

"I remember the very day that I became colored," Zora Neale Hurston wrote of the day she left the all-black town where she grew up. "I left Eatonville, the town of the oleanders, as Zora. When I disembarked from the river-boat at Jacksonville, she was no more. It seemed that I had suffered a sea change. I was not Zora of Orange County any more, I was now a little colored girl."

Hurston refused to be cast as "tragically colored." And so this new identity was, she maintained, simply a change in consciousness, at worst a discomfort. "No," she wrote, "I do not weep at the world—I am too busy sharpening my oyster knife."

Perhaps it is only through leaving home that you can learn who you are. Or at least who the world thinks you are. And the gap between the one and the other is the painful part, the part that you may, if you are me, or if you are Zora Neale Hurston, keep arguing against for the rest of your life—saying, *No, I am not white in* that *way,* or, *No, I am not black in* that *way.*

I used to say that I did not realize I was white until I moved to New York City, but that is not true. I knew full well by then that I was white. What I realized in New York was what it feels like to be an outsider in your own home, and that is not what it means to be white in this country.

"Nobody knows me," I cried to my mother on the phone during that first year in New York. My days were infused with the isolation and the paranoia of an outsider. I remember, for instance, my persistent suspicion that the little boys in Fort Greene Park peed when they saw me coming. At my most clearheaded, I understood that the boys just happened to have a pissing game and that I just happened to walk through the park while they were at it. But still, I was nagged by the possibility that the pissing was a message to me, a message that I was unequipped to interpret as an outsider but that I guessed meant, "We piss on you and your whiteness."

Along with several boxes of documents about Buxton, there is, in the archives at the University of Iowa library, a series of oral histories documenting the lives of women from Latino communities in Iowa. Some of these communities date back to the 1880s, to boxcar towns next to railroad yards. And some of the oral histories read—in their incomplete form, because they have not yet been typed by someone who understands Spanish—"My father was born in XXXX in Mexico. His name was Jose XXXX. His mother was XXXXXX." Some include summary: "After fifteen years in Iowa, Carmen feels that she has achieved the community's respect." Some ache: "I came here without my family, without my climate, without my mountains and without my culture."

The town of Cook's Point was a small Mexican American community near the city of Davenport, Iowa. It was next to the town dump, on land formerly occupied by lumber mills and owned by a "liquidation corporation." Cook's Point had no pavement or drainage, and its tarpaper shacks were leveled after the land was sold to an industrial developer in the 1940s. One old woman, the local newspaper reported, remained rocking on her porch as the bulldozers approached, and another family remained in two rooms of their house even as bulldozers ripped off the other half.

A sense of home is, it seems, worth more than any other comfort. And one of the questions I want to answer now, for myself, is what makes a place feel like home. I know that it is not so simple as living where people speak your language and look like you and have lost what you have lost, but there is a kind of comfort in that, too.

An economic survey of Cook's Point conducted before it was razed revealed, among other things, that the people who lived there were probably not as poor as their conditions might have suggested. The average income in Cook's Point was very close to the national average. Some families there had savings in the bank, and life insurance, and health insurance, and a number of families owned cars. The people of Cook's Point did not have access—because they were squatting on land they did not own, in a place that was not formally a town—to municipal utilities like running water and electricity, but after Cook's Point was bulldozed and the people who lived there were forced to integrate into Davenport and Moline and Silvis, many bought homes and led middle-class lives. What they lost in the process is recorded in oral histories riddled with Xs.

"I had been raised in a white surrounding," Lola Reeves said of moving to Buxton from a town where her family was one of three black families. "Going to Buxton with all the people of my own race was a great experience for me. . . . I could exercise my feelings, my potentials, my talent and my social life and I think Buxton brought a whole lot of joy to me, just to be able to live and, a colored girl, in a colored area and feeling like I was one of them and I was happy."

And perhaps this is part of why integration in this country remains as troubled and as incomplete as ever. In 1955, Zora Neale Hurston was among those who opposed the Supreme Court decision to integrate public schools in the South. "The whole matter revolves around the self-respect of my people," she wrote. "How much satisfaction can I get from a court order for somebody to associate with me who does not wish me near them?" The forcible integration of schools on the grounds of offering a better education to black students was, she felt, an insult to black teachers. "It is a contradiction in terms," she wrote, "to scream race pride and equality while at the same time spurning Negro teachers and self-association."

What integration seems to mean to many white people is that a very small number of other people will be accepted into white communities and institutions, where they will be "tolerated." I suspect that Hurston, an anthropologist, a collector of culture, understood the implications of this. Assimilation is the unspoken end. But I would like to believe that this country is capable of a version of integration greater, more ambitious, than that.

I found myself wondering, as I read the report on diversity at the University of Iowa, whom this particular version of diversity was serving and whom it was intended to serve. For whose sake, I wondered, did the university want to increase the number of minority students from 9 percent to 10.9 percent? It did not seem to be for the sake of those students, for the sake of their education, or for the sake of their selves. I suspected that it was more for the sake of the institution, so that it could appear properly progressive. Or perhaps it was for the sake of the white students, so that they might be exposed to a limited degree of diversity and thus be made more worldly. This might help explain some of the disappointment of the minority students who arrived at the university only to find that they were in service to the education of others.

One of the mysteries of Buxton is why Consolidated Coal so actively participated in creating and maintaining a substantially black town in Iowa. The scholars who studied Buxton could not answer this question. The most cynical explanation, that Consolidated wanted to divide its workforce to undermine their collective power, is contradicted not only by the fact that all the miners belonged to the same union, but also by the experiences of the people who lived in Buxton. Many of them believed that the company actively discouraged discrimination, both public and private, and that a man could lose his job for spitting on another man.

Whatever the explanation, there was coal to mine in Buxton, but there were also lives to lead, and somehow both undertakings turned out all right for a while. It is naive, I think, to suppose that Buxton was truly a utopia. But I would still like to believe what one man who used to live there said, decades after he left: "I'm not so sure, I'm not so sure you can't go back to Buxton."

Is This Kansas

The girls were wearing nothing but white towels and high heels. There were about thirty of them, and they passed in an animated swarm like one of those flocks of white pelicans that can occasionally be seen migrating through the Midwest with sun silvering off their wings. I was returning from a walk by the river and I stopped there on the sidewalk to stare after the clatter and gaggle of the girls. The rituals of that town, a town in which the population doubles while the university is in session, became only more foreign to me the longer I stayed. The chanting on sorority lawns, the parades, the groups in matching T-shirts that read "Pharmacy Bar Crawl '06" or "Ted's Birthday!" The shivering girls hugging themselves and clicking down the streets bare-shouldered and drunk in February, the endless game played with beanbags on front lawns, the boys roving at night after the bars closed, hollering. The car crashes, the falls from balconies, the alcohol poisonings. The football game days, on which cars crept toward the stadium in long, slow lines and everyone wore black and gold. The empty plastic cups under bushes, the idle boys on decaying porches, the midnight Ping-Pong tournaments, the windows illuminated by neon beer signs.

I would often wonder, during my time in that town, why, of all the subcultures in the United States that are feared and hated, of all the subcultures that are singled out as morally reprehensible or un-American or criminal, student culture is so pardoned. Illinois home owners propose ordinances against shared housing among immigrants, while their sons are at college sharing one-bedroom apartments with five other boys. Courts send black teenagers to jail for possession of marijuana, while white college kids are sentenced with community service for driving while intoxicated, a considerably more deadly offense. And Evangelicals editorialize about the sexual abominations of consenting adults, while very little is said about the plague of date rapes in college towns.

One reason for all this might involve the sign on Liberty Bank in downtown Iowa City that reads "Welcome Students!" Or perhaps it has more to do with the fact that those of us who own homes, and those of us who write laws, who demand ordinances from the city council, who lead congregations, see students not as Trojan soldiers hiding in the wooden horse of education, but as the quickly dying sparks of our former selves. And so we allow them their romp, believing that beer pong will lose its luster after four years and that these students will graduate, most likely, into a life of harmless drudgery, in which they will cease drinking loudly and begin drinking more quietly, quickly becoming the kind of thick, docile citizens the Midwest expects them to become.

One August in Iowa City, on the day when student leases traditionally expire and lamps and mattresses are piled into borrowed horse trailers or minivans or pickup trucks while crippled dressers without drawers and legless chairs are left by the curb, an alarming pile of couches appeared on the corner of Iowa and Summit. There were ten or fifteen couches in the pile, and it was nearly twenty feet tall. It came to a kind of jagged peak, as if intended for a flag. The couches in that pile were still redolent of the homes from which they had been torn, from the suburbs of Chicago or the farms of Iowa, and the old hopes and ambitions of those places. They were tastefully floral or conservatively brown, and one, I remember, near the top, had a tiny pineapple pattern just like my own Midwestern grandparents' couch. But these couches were scarred with cigarette burns and smelled, after the rain that came the next day, of vomit. The pile of couches stood for a week or so like a monument to the city, a monument to the sad waste of it. It was a reminder that this place was not wholesome, as the Midwest likes to imagine itself, but rather perverse.

In the spring before the pile of couches arrived, I became accustomed to visiting, at one or two in the morning, the weekday parties on my block and informing the hosts that I lived three houses down, or five houses down, that I was their neighbor, and that I could not sleep because of their music. I considered this a kind of public service, because there were just as many families and working people on my block as there were students. After one such visit to a party where I arrived to find a grown man suspended upside down by several boys who seemed to be occupied with siphoning beer into the man through a tube, I returned the next day to thank the boys for how quickly they had shut down the party. They invited me inside, and their screen door clanged behind me in their dim living room, where they stood on their miserable, sticky floor with their baseball caps pulled over their eyes, looking at their feet and calling me ma'am. The boy I had spoken to the night before took pains to tell me that he had wanted to end the party earlier but that some of his friends had brought their parents, and that it had been especially hard to persuade the parents to go home.

There are nearly as many churches in Iowa City as there are bars, and one of the many Christian concepts that my students introduced me to during my time as a graduate instructor at the University of Iowa was the idea that one must love the sinner but hate the sin. Having absorbed something of my father's great reverence for knowledge, and being aware that less than a third of the people in my country could ever expect a bachelor's degree, I was tempted to believe that to waste a college education was a sin. But I knew that my students were not being offered the kind of education I had enjoyed as an undergraduate. That was a much more expensive education, and, while it might not have been better, it was more indulgent. I also knew that my students were not all wasting their education and that some were waiting tables or installing air conditioners to pay for it. I knew that I owed them a complicated debt. Their tuition was being used to pay me to learn how to teach college students. They were preparing me for a career, and I could not with any confidence say that I was doing the same for them.

The philosophy of education that dominated the University of Iowa, an ideology not unlike the thinking that dominates many other universities, seemed not only to encourage but to depend on the quiet resignation of the students. That is not to say that there were not excellent professors at the university or that the students were without opportunities. But they were at the bottom of an immense hierarchy that was preoccupied with many concerns other than their education. One didn't need to spend very long at that institution before realizing that the interests of everyone else—the funders, the administrators, the professors, the graduate students—came before the interests of the undergraduate students. And as in any feudal system, the people on whom the entire system depended were robbed, as completely as possible, of their power. The students were, for the most part, unable to hold inept teachers accountable, to protest the wasting of their own time, to influence the grounds on which they would be evaluated, to demand anything, really, of substance from the institution. There were procedures for such things, of course, but they consisted mostly of misleading paperwork. The students were subjects of this education, which was acted out upon them. They either absorbed it or did not.

As a graduate student, I enjoyed much greater autonomy than the undergraduate students whom I was paid to teach, but I found the philosophy of education in which I was immersed so distasteful that I absorbed very little of that education myself. I was impatient and argumentative in the classroom. I was the very kind of student whom I now dread, who I fear will reveal to me how dependent I have become on the hollow authority of my place in the institution. Often sleepless, I was in the habit of writing angry letters at midnight, and I became a burr in the already messy hair of the English Department. On one occasion, my complaints made the head of the English Department, a former military man, very red in the face, and he stabbed his finger at me, calling me a "presumptuous young lady." I was stunned not so much by the finger in my face as by what it meant. I was no longer an adult there, but a child again. And so, reduced to the frustrated tantrums of a powerless child, I raged my way through my education at Iowa, while my students, whose Midwestern dispositions did not so readily allow for sober displays of rage, drank their way through it.

On the first day of the very first class I taught at the university, I told my students that I had lived in New York City for a few years, where I had taught creative writing to elementary school and high school students. I told them this as evidence that I had some teaching experience, to compensate for what I understood to be my grave underqualifications for my job as their instructor. But they weren't as interested in my inadequacies as they were in New York City. They wanted to know where I had lived there, and where I had worked, and if I had been scared. They wanted to know if men had harassed me. I told them that, yes, men had harassed me on the street, but no more than the frat boys in Iowa City harassed me as I walked past their houses. In fact, I told them, I found Lucas Street on a Thursday night, with all the hooting from dim porches and the boys smashing beer cans, to be significantly scarier than anywhere I had ever been in New York. They didn't quite believe me, but I was telling the truth. And this was before a drunk frat boy broke into my apartment two weekends in a row, the first time wearing Mardi Gras beads and passing out just inside the front door, the second time becoming belligerent and refusing to leave until the police arrived. This was also before a group of students on my street dragged a couch out of their house in the middle of the night and used it to barricade my neighbor's door so that she could not get out, and then sat on it, ignoring her screams until the police arrived. This neighbor, who didn't eat meat because she couldn't bear the thought of harming animals, would then buy a pellet gun for self-defense. Iowa City remains, to this day, the only place I have ever lived where I have had reason to speak with the police with any regularity.

Racism, I would discover during my first semester teaching at Iowa, does not exist. At least not in Iowa. Not in the minds of the twenty-three tall, healthy, blond students to whom I was supposed to teach rhetoric. And not, at least not publicly, in the opinion of the one student who did not look white but who promptly informed the class that she was adopted and considered herself white.

Sexism does not exist either, at least not anymore. My students considered my interest in these subjects very antiquated. These things, they informed me with exasperation, had already been resolved a long time ago, during the sixties. In the course of one of our discussions about the rhetoric of the gay-marriage controversy, several students agreed that it would be a good idea to send all of the gay people in America to one state, one largely unpopulated state, like North Dakota, where they could live together and send their children to schools that would be "separate but equal." I asked them if they knew that the Supreme Court had found the concept of separate but equal inherently flawed. No, they reported innocently, they did not know.

Their ignorance, I would come to believe, was not entirely their fault. These were students just out of high school, where they had been taught that the world was benign and that hard work and obedience would inevitably be rewarded with prosperity. Their complacency in maintaining that myth was willful, but it was also somewhat necessary to the lives they were expected to lead.

Hurricane Katrina touched down in Louisiana the week after classes started in my last year of teaching at the University of Iowa. I was on my way to a funeral when Michael Chertoff told Robert Siegel on the radio, "I have not heard a report of thousands of people in the convention center who don't have food and water." I watched the floodwaters lapping rooftops on the television in a house where an only child was mourning the loss of her mother. As I was already wearing black, and as I was waiting to leave for the funeral home while I watched the news, I was well prepared to regard the situation in New Orleans as I would a death in the family. Perhaps that is why I was shocked when I returned to find so many people on campus preoccupied not with the flooding of New Orleans but with the looting of New Orleans. My students, in particular, kept saying of the looting, "Well, that's where I draw the line." What line that was,

I did not ask. But I supposed it was the line between victim and villain. Because white Americans have tended, for hundreds of years now, to think of black Americans as either victims or villains—children or savages.

A week after the levees broke, *Boston Globe* columnist Jeff Jacoby was describing the people of New Orleans as "predators," "primitives," and "savages." "Those who called early on for shooting looters on sight should have been listened to," Jacoby wrote, "not because property is more valuable than human life, but because when property isn't safe from marauders, human life isn't, either." This impossible equation equaled out, of course, only if one was willing to assume that some human lives are more valuable than others. This, in the name of "morality."

When looting broke out in New Orleans, America suddenly became a moral nation. A nation concerned with what was, philosophically speaking, "right." Now, while people were waiting in the Superdome for the government to fulfill its most basic duty toward its citizens, everyone from the Associated Press to Fox News was interested in examining the ethics of stealing during a crisis. Those of us who balked at this false piousness were accused of moral equivalence, like the Syracuse University professor who told Alan Colmes, "You need to talk about the issues. The fact is that you're choosing one segment of society to kick around. You've got looters with Enron. You've got looters in Iraq. Focus on that. Talk about that."

America also quite suddenly became a nation capable of distinguishing between necessities and luxuries. My students, many of whom regularly spent the money their parents sent them for food on alcohol, became adamant on this point, the

damning point in the debate over the looting in New Orleans—
the fact that some people were not taking just food and water
from stores, but also alcohol and televisions.

At the time, I simply widened my eyes and said nothing. The
discussion, it was clear, was not so much a discussion as it was
an extended metaphor. We were not talking about looting, we
were talking about everything white Americans feared would be
taken from us by black Americans. The metaphor did not end
with looting, of course, because fear moves like floodwaters. The
reports of looting in New Orleans came mingled with reports of
fantastic acts of violence—children with their throats slit and babies raped. These stories would later be exposed as false. Within
a few weeks of the first reports of violence, the *Times-Picayune*
and then the *Los Angeles Times* and the *New York Times* and the
Washington Post would all run articles correcting the record, revealing that most, if not all, of the incidents of violence they had
reported in the aftermath of Katrina had been myths.

In one popular correction, the superintendent of the New
Orleans Police Department, who had been quoted in the *New
York Times* as saying, "The tourists are walking around there,
and as soon as these individuals see them, they're being preyed
upon. They are beating, they are raping them in the streets,"
would clarify that this statement was based on rumors and that
"we have no official reports to document any murder. Not one
official report of rape or sexual assault." The relief helicopter
that had famously been shot at from the ground, it was revealed,
was not actually shot at. Young girls had not been found with
their throats slit. And the babies who were in reality suffering
from a lack of food and water were not, in reality, being raped.

But, as the philosopher Slavoj Žižek would observe, false reports of violence had already corrupted rescue efforts by the time they were corrected. "They generated fears that caused some police officers to quit and led the authorities to change troop deployments, delay medical evacuations and ground helicopters," Žižek wrote. "Acadian Ambulance Company, for example, locked down its cars after word came that armed robbers had looted all of the water from a firehouse in Covington—a report that proved totally untrue."

Our willingness to imagine our own people as villains, as savages, is not a private problem of unclean thinking. It is an issue of public safety. And it should not take a rash of factual errors in our newspapers to make this clear. Even if all the reports of violence following Katrina had been true, the story that was made of them would still be problematic. Because in this case the story preceded the facts, instead of emerging from them. And the story—that blacks are violent barbarians—was already far too old to qualify as news.

Unlike the reports of violence, many of the reports of looting in New Orleans were, in fact, substantiated. There were witnesses and photographs. But, again, the story—that blacks are thieves—was already in circulation before the events took place. The facts of the reports may have been true, but the motives driving the reporting, and the motives behind the public fascination with the story, were based on old lies about who steals from whom in this country. And it was evident from the strange enthusiasm, the eagerness, with which those reports of looting were met that readers were not interested so much in the looting as they were in how well it supported their sickest suspicions of black people. Our willingness to believe the news is, in many cases, not entirely innocent.

About six months after the levees broke in New Orleans, Iowa City was visited by a storm of its own. On a Thursday evening in April, a tornado roared directly through downtown Iowa City, collapsing St. Patrick's Church, ripping a wall off the Liquor House, and leaving by way of Iowa Avenue, where it lifted the roof off a sorority house and spun cars into a ravine and ravaged several blocks of houses.

A girl who had been hiding under a table in the sorority house would later describe the tornado as sounding like a "freight train," a description that means something in Iowa City, where freight trains pass through town regularly, rattling the windows of classrooms and pausing conversations and haunting the night with their whistles. In all, a thousand houses were damaged. Trees and traffic signals and power lines were torn down. And in the dark silence after the storm the streets filled with students carrying plastic cups of beer and digital cameras, wandering past the live wires and the gas leaks, and lighting cigarettes. Some students dragged a couch into the street and sat on it, while some others gathered around cases of beer in a parking lot.

"After the funnel went through town, but while sirens were still sounding," the Cedar Rapids *Gazette* reported the next day, "college students in the rental neighborhoods around downtown made their way onto the sidewalks and streets by the hundreds. Those who were already in the bars downtown came outside." It was a version of the usual Thursday-night carnival, but set against the backdrop, this time, of disaster. And that backdrop revealed the carnival for what it was. "Posing by the downed power lines and overturned cars, cheesing for their cameras and cell phones," the opinion editor for the *Iowa City Press-Citizen* wrote, "the onlookers seemed to view the damaged downtown as an amusement park—walking through the storm's path of destruction like it was a new adventure ride."

The sound of chain saws began the morning after the storm and did not stop for months. Windows were boarded over, and spray-painted messages appeared on the streets. On a piece of plywood on Iowa Avenue: "Don't Gawk, Help." And on the boarded-over window of a barbershop, in orange spray paint: "Toto, is this Kansas?"

The local newspapers reported the looting very cautiously. The *Press-Citizen* described it only as "small-scale looting." The *Gazette* mentioned only that "some scattered reports, most unconfirmed, of looting were made." The student newspaper, the *Daily Iowan,* was more specific: "Curious passersby took advantage of the chance to swipe a few free beers from smashed and damaged stores and convenience stations—incidents that many gas-station operators throughout Iowa City's nucleus reported. 'The Liquor House opened up like a can of tuna, and all my neighbors ran up and started taking liquor,' said UI senior Sam Ehlinger as he meandered through the Pedestrian Mall around 10 p.m. Thursday." But when asked to confirm this story by the *Daily Iowan* reporter, the employees at the Liquor House declined to comment. "Now's not the time," said one.

The looting would cease to be a story very quickly, giving

way to the story the town preferred to tell itself. As the *Gazette* put it, "It never fails that a wicked Midwestern storm brings out the wonderful Midwestern compassion for our neighbors. Amid a few reports of looting, the most prevalent scene after tornadoes and thunderstorms caused a big mess last week was that of neighbor helping neighbor."

Meanwhile, my students told me about drinking thirty-packs of beer in parking lots after the storm had passed, and they told me about watching their friends throw bricks through windows, about sitting on mattresses on front lawns, watching the National Guard come in, and about the kegger in the Pentacrest Apartments. When I asked them what they had learned from the storm, one student said, after a moment of grave and woeful reflection, "I guess you never know how you're going to act in a situation until you're in it."

Iowa City is a small city, and the storm that hit it was a small storm. The incident barely made national news, meriting only one brief mention in the *New York Times*. And so it was sobering for me to watch, as the months passed and the houses on Iowa Avenue still stood vacant, how difficult it was for the town to recover. And how different spring looked with half as many trees. When I left Iowa City three months after the storm, small scraps of metal and bits of insulation were still hanging in some branches. Blue tarps covered roofs on Iowa Avenue. A bull-dozer stood idle on the lawn of the sorority that had lost its roof and a wall. But the students, the victims and the villains of that place, were still sitting on their porches, still tossing beanbags on Jefferson Street, and still drinking.

No Man's Land

"What is it about water that always affects a person?" Laura Ingalls Wilder wrote in her 1894 diary. "I never see a great river or lake but I think how I would like to see a world made and watch it through all its changes."

Forty years later, she would reflect that she had "seen the whole frontier, the woods, the Indian country of the great plains, the frontier towns, the building of the railroads in wild unsettled country, homesteading and farmers coming in to take possession." She realized, she said, that she "had seen and lived it all."

It was a world made and unmade. And it was not without some ambivalence, not without some sense of loss, that Laura Ingalls Wilder the writer watched the Indians, as many as she could see in either direction, ride out of the Kansas of her imagination. Her fictional self, the Laura of *Little House on the Prairie,* sobbed as they left.

Like my sister, like my cousin, like so many other girls, I was captivated, in my childhood, by that Laura. I was given a bonnet, and I wore it earnestly for quite some time, in the sun and in the shade. But that reveals how little I knew the Laura I loved. She hated her bonnet, which her mother told her to wear so that she would not become "brown as an Indian."

When I return to *Little House on the Prairie* now, as an adult, I find that it is not the book I thought it was. It is not the gauzy frontier fantasy I made of it as a child. It is not a naive celebration of the American pioneer. It is the document of a woman interrogating her legacy. It is, as the scholar Ann Romines has called it, "one of our most disturbing and ambitious narratives about failures and experiments of acculturation in the American West."

In that place and time where one world was ending and another was beginning, in that borderland between conflicting claims, the fictional Laura, the child of the frontier, struggles through her story. She hides, she cowers, she rages, she cries. She asks, "Will the government make these Indians go west?" and she asks, "Won't it make the Indians mad to have to —" but then she is cut off and told to go to sleep. She falls ill and wakes from a fever to find a black doctor attending her. She picks up beads at an abandoned Indian camp and strings them for her sister. She lusts after a "half-breed." The real Laura grows up riding back and forth in covered wagons across the Middle West, passing through immigrant towns and towns where she notes in her diary seeing "a great many colored people." She marries a farmer named Almanzo and settles, finally, in the Ozarks.

Up until her death, Laura Ingalls Wilder would not allow a fence to be built around her house. She loved the land enough to know exactly what had been stolen to make her world. "If I had been the Indians," she wrote in her 1894 diary, as she looked out over a river and some bluffs in South Dakota, "I would have scalped more white folks before I ever would have left it."

ON THE BORDER

Shortly after we married, my husband and I moved to a part of Chicago that was once known as No Man's Land. At the turn of the century, when Chicago had already burned and been re-built again, this was still a sandy forest of birch and oak trees. It was the sparsely populated place between the city of Chicago and the city of Evanston, the place just north of the boundary that once designated Indian Territory, a place where the streets were unpaved and unlighted.

Now this neighborhood is called Rogers Park, and the city blocks of Chicago, all paved and lighted, run directly into the city blocks of Evanston, with only a cemetery to mark the boundary between the two municipalities. The Chicago trains end here, and the tracks turn back in a giant loop around the gravel yard where idle trains are docked. Seven blocks to the east of the train station is the shore of Lake Michigan, which rolls and crashes past the horizon, reminding us, with its winds and spray, that we are on the edge of something vast.

There are a dozen empty storefronts on Howard Avenue be-tween the lake and the train station—a closed Chinese restau-rant, a closed dry cleaner, a closed thrift shop, a closed hot-dog place. There is an open Jamaican restaurant, a Caribbean American bakery, a liquor store, a shoe store, and several little grocery markets. Women push baby carriages here, little boys eat bags of chips in front of the markets, and men smoke outside the train station while the trains rattle the air.

We moved to Chicago because I was hired to teach at the university in Evanston, which is within walking distance of Rogers Park. Walking to campus along the lakeshore for the first time, I passed the cemetery and then a block of brick apartment buildings much like the ones on my block, and then I began to pass houses with gables and turrets and stone walls and copper gutters and huge bay windows and manicured lawns and circular drives. I passed beaches where sailboats were pulled up on the sand, where canoes and kayaks were stacked, I passed fountains, I passed parks with willow trees, I passed through one block that was gated at both ends. I passed signs that read, "Private Road, No Access, Police Enforced."

Evanston was still an officially segregated city in 1958 when Martin Luther King spoke there about the Greek concept of agape, love for all humanity. On my first visit to Evanston, after my job interview, I experienced a moment of panic during which I stood with the big, cool stone buildings of the university and its lawns and trees behind me while I called my sister to tell her that I was afraid that this might not be the life for me. I was afraid, I told her, that if I became a professor I would be forever cloistered here, forever insulated from the rest of the world. My sister, who is herself training to be a professor, was not moved. There are worse fates, she reminded me.

Of the seventy-seven official "community areas" of Chicago, twenty-four are populated by over 90 percent of one race, and only twelve have no racial majority. Rogers Park is one of those few. It is celebrated as the most diverse neighborhood in a hypersegregated city. By the time I moved to Rogers Park, quite a few people had already warned me about the place. Two of them were my colleagues at the university, who both made mention of gangs. Others were near strangers, like my sister's roommate's mother, who asked her daughter to call me on the day I was packing my moving truck to share her suspicion that I might be moving somewhere dangerous. And then there was my mother, who grew up in a western suburb of Chicago but has, for almost twenty years now, lived in an old farmhouse in rural New York. She told me she had heard from someone that the neighborhood I was moving to might not be safe, that there were gangs there. "Ma," I said to her, "what do you know about gangs?" And she said, "I know enough—I know that they're out there." Which is about as much as I know, and about as much as most white folks who talk about gangs seem to know, which is to say nothing.

IN THE IMAGINATION

Gangs are real, but they are also conceptual. The word "gang" is frequently used to avoid using the word "black" in a way that might be offensive. For instance, by pairing it with a suggestion of fear.

My cousin recently traveled to South Africa, where someone with her background would typically be considered neither white nor black but colored, a distinct racial group in South Africa. Her skin is light enough that she was most often taken to be white, which was something she was prepared for, having traveled in other parts of Africa. But she was not prepared for what it meant to be white in South Africa, which was to be reminded, at every possible opportunity, that she was not safe and that she must be afraid. And she was not prepared for how seductive that fear would become, how omnipresent it would be, so she spent most of her time there in taxis, and in hotels, and in "safe" places where she was surrounded by white people. When she returned home she told me, "I realized this is what white people do to each other—they cultivate each other's fear. It's very violent."

We are afraid, my husband suggests, because we have guilty consciences. We secretly suspect that we might have more than we deserve. We know that white folks have reaped some ill-gotten gains in this country. And so privately, quietly, as a result of our own complicated guilt, we believe that we deserve to be hated, to be hurt, and to be killed.

But, for the most part, we are not. Most victims of violent crimes are not white. This is particularly true for "hate" crimes. We are far more likely to be hurt by the food we eat, the cars we drive, or the bicycles we ride than by the people we live among. This may be lost on us in part because we are surrounded by a lot of noise that suggests otherwise. Within the past month, for example, the *Chicago Tribune* reported on an "unprovoked stabbing spree," a "one-man crime wave," a boy who was beaten in a park, and a bartender who was beaten behind her bar, the story being, again and again, that none of us are safe in this city.

IN THE CITY

In the spring of 2006, the *New York Times* published an analysis of all the murders that had been committed in New York City during the previous three years—a total of 1,662 murders. The article revealed one trend: people who were murdered tended to be murdered by other people like them. Most of the killers were men and boys (a disturbing 93 percent—a number that, if we weren't so accustomed to thinking of men as "naturally" violent, might strike us as the symptom of an alarming mass pathology), and most killed other men and boys. In more than three-fourths of the killings, the killer and the victim were of the same race, and less than 13 percent of the victims were white or Asian. The majority of children were killed by a parent, and in more than half of all the cases, the victim and the killer knew each other.

Even as it made this point, the article undid its own message by detailing a series of stranger-murders. There was the serial murderer who shot shopkeepers, the KFC customer who stabbed a cashier, the man who offered a ride to a group of strangers and was then murdered for his car. These are the murders we find most compelling, of course, because these are the murders that allow us to be afraid of the people we want to be afraid of.

In a similar layering of popular fantasy with true information, the article went on to mention specific precincts in Brooklyn, the Bronx, and Harlem where murders were concentrated, and then quoted Andrew Karmen, an expert in victimology, who explained, "The problem of crime and violence is rooted in neighborhood conditions—high rates of poverty, family disruption, failing schools, lack of recreational opportunities, active recruitment by street gangs, drug markets. People forced to reside under those conditions are at a greater risk of getting caught up in violence, as victims or as perpetrators." In other words, particular neighborhoods are not as dangerous as the conditions within those neighborhoods. It's a fine line but an important one, because if you don't live in those conditions, you aren't very likely to get killed. Not driving through, not walking through, not even renting an apartment.

I worked, during my first year in New York, in some of the city's most notorious neighborhoods: in Bed-Stuy, in East New York, in Spanish Harlem, in Washington Heights. That was before I knew the language of the city, and the codes, so I had no sense that these places were considered dangerous. I was hired by the parks department to inspect community gardens, and I traveled all over the city, on train and on bus and on foot, wearing khaki shorts and hiking boots, carrying a clipboard and a Polaroid camera.

I did not understand then that city blocks on which most of the lots were empty or full of the rubble of collapsed buildings would be read, by many New Yorkers, as an indication of danger. I understood that these places were poverty-stricken and ripe with ambient desperation, but I did not suspect that they were any more dangerous than anywhere else in the city. I was accustomed to the semirural poverty and postindustrial decay of upstate New York. There, by the highways, yards are piled with broken plastic and rusting metal, tarps are tacked on in place of walls, roof beams are slowly rotting through. And in the small cities, in Troy and Watervliet, in Schenectady and Niskayuna, in Amsterdam and in parts of Albany, old brick buildings crumble, brownstones stand vacant, and factories with huge windows wait to be gutted and razed.

Beyond the rumor that the old hot-dog factory was haunted, I don't remember any mythology of danger clinging to the landscape of upstate New York. And the only true horror story I had ever heard about New York City before I moved there was the story of my grandmother's brother, a farm boy who had gone to the city and died of gangrene after cutting his bare foot on some dirty glass. "Please," my grandmother begged me with tears in her eyes before I moved to New York, "always wear your shoes."

And I did. But by the time I learned what I was really supposed to be afraid of in New York, I knew better—which isn't to say that there was nothing to be afraid of, because, as all of us know, there are always dangers, everywhere.

But danger was an abstraction to me then, not something I felt. In fact, I can recall vividly the first time I made the intellectual deduction that I might be in a dangerous situation—I was riding the subway in Manhattan well past midnight, and I noticed after just a few minutes on the train that I was the only woman in that car. At the next stop, I walked into the next car, which was also full of men, and so I began traveling the length of the train. I eventually found a car where a woman was sleeping with her head resting on the man next to her, but by then I was unsettled. I looked into other trains as they passed us in the tunnels, and I looked at the people waiting on the platforms.

Women did not ride the subway alone very late at night, I realized. And as I made this realization I felt not fear, but fury.

Even now, at a much more wary and guarded age, what I feel when I am told that my neighborhood is dangerous is not fear but anger at the extent to which so many of us have agreed to live within a delusion—namely, that we will be spared the dangers that others suffer only if we move within certain very restricted spheres, and that insularity is a fair price to pay for safety.

Fear is isolating for those that fear. And I have come to believe that fear is a cruelty to those who are feared. I once met a man of pro-football-sized proportions who saw something in my hesitation when I shook his hand that inspired him to tell me he was pained by the way small women looked at him when he passed them on the street—pained by the fear in their eyes, pained by the way they drew away—and as he told me this, tears welled up in his eyes.

One evening not long after we moved to Rogers Park, my husband and I met a group of black boys riding their bikes on the sidewalk across the street from our apartment building. The boys were weaving down the sidewalk, yelling for the sake of hearing their own voices and drinking from forty-ounce bottles of beer. As we stepped off the sidewalk and began crossing the street toward our apartment, one boy yelled, "Don't be afraid of us!" I looked back over my shoulder as I stepped into the street, and the boy passed on his bike so that I saw him looking back at me also, and then he yelled again, directly at me, "Don't be afraid of us!"

I wanted to yell back, "Don't worry, we aren't!" but I was, in fact, afraid to engage the boys, afraid to draw attention to my husband and myself, afraid of how my claim not to be afraid might be misunderstood as bravado begging a challenge, so I simply let my eyes meet the boy's eyes before I turned, disturbed, toward the tall iron gate in front of my apartment building, a gate that gives the appearance of being locked but is in fact always open.

IN THE WATER

My love of swimming in open water, in lakes and oceans, is tempered only by my fear of what I cannot see beneath those waters. My mind imagines into the depths a nightmare landscape of grabbing hands and spinning metal blades and dark, sucking voids into which I will be pulled and not return. As a charm against my terror of the unseen, I have, for many years now, always entered the water silently repeating to myself this command: *Trust the water.* And for some time after an incident in which one of my feet brushed the other and I swam for shore frantically in a gasping panic, breathing water in the process and choking painfully, I added: *Don't be afraid of your own feet.*

I am accustomed to being warned away from the water, to being told that it is too cold, too deep, too rocky, that the current is too strong and the waves are too powerful. Until recently, what I learned from these warnings was only that I could safely defy them all. But then I was humbled by a rough beach in northern California, where I was slammed to the bottom by the surf and dragged to shore so forcefully that sand was embedded in the skin of my palms and my knees. That beach happened to have had a sign that read "How to Survive This Beach," which made me laugh when I first arrived, the first item in the numbered list being, "Do not go within 500 feet of the water."

It is only since I have discovered that some warnings are legitimate that my fears of open water have become powerful enough to fight my confidence in my own strength. I tend to stay closer to shore now, and I am always vigilant, although for what, exactly, I do not know. It is difficult to know what to be afraid of and how cautious to be when there are so many imagined dangers in the world, so many killer sharks, and so many creatures from the Black Lagoon.

Now that we share a bookshelf, I am in possession of my husband's dog-eared, underlined copy of Barry Glassner's *The Culture of Fear*. Every society is threatened by a nearly infinite amount of dangers, Glassner writes, but societies differ in what they choose to fear. Americans, interestingly, tend to be most preoccupied with those dangers that are among the least likely to cause us harm, while we ignore the problems that are hurting the greatest number of people. We suffer from a national confusion between true threats and imagined threats.

And our imagined threats, Glassner argues, very often serve to mask true threats. Quite a bit of noise, for example, is made about the minuscule risk that our children might be molested by strange pedophiles, while in reality most children who are sexually molested are molested by close relatives in their own homes. The greatest risk factor for these children is not the proximity of a pedophile or a pervert, but the poverty in which they tend to live. And the sensationalism around our "war" on illegal drugs has obscured the fact that legal drugs, the kind of drugs that are advertised on television, are more widely abused and cause more deaths than illegal drugs. Worse than this, we allow our misplaced, illogical fears to stigmatize our own people. "Fear mongers," Glassner writes, "project onto black men precisely what slavery, poverty, educational deprivation, and discrimination have ensured that they do not have—great power and influence."

Although I do not pretend to understand the full complexity of local economies, I suspect that fear is one of the reasons that I can afford to live where I live, in an apartment across the street from a beach, with a view of the lake and space enough for both my husband and me to have rooms in which to write. Our lake home, we sometimes call it, with a wink to the fact that this apartment is far better than we ever believed two writers with student loan debt and one income could hope for. As one Chicago real-estate magazine puts it: "For decades, a low rate of owner occupancy, a lack of commercial development . . . and problems with crime have kept prices lower in East Rogers Park than in many North Side neighborhoods." And so my feelings about fear are somewhat ambivalent, because fear is why I can afford to swim every day now.

One of the paradoxes of our time is that the War on Terror has served mainly to reinforce a collective belief that maintaining the right amount of fear and suspicion will earn one safety. Fear is promoted by the government as a kind of policy. Fear is accepted, even among the best-educated people in this country, even among the professors with whom I work, as a kind of intelligence. And inspiring fear in others is often seen as neighborly and kindly, instead of being regarded as what my cousin recognized it for—a violence.

On my first day in Rogers Park, my downstairs neighbors, a family of European immigrants whom I met on my way out to swim, warned me that a boy had drowned by the breakwater not too long ago. I was in my bathing suit when they told me this, holding a towel. And, they told me, another neighbor, walking his dog on the beach, had recently found a human arm. It was part of the body of a boy who had been killed in gang warfare and then cut up with a tree saw. The torso was found later, they told me, farther up the shore, but the head was never found.

I went for my swim, avoiding the breakwater and pressing back a new terror of heads with open mouths at the bottom of the lake. When I retold the neighbors' story to my husband later, he laughed. "A tree saw?" he asked, still laughing.

ON THE FRONTIER

When the Irish immigrant Philip Rogers built a log cabin nine miles north of the Chicago courthouse in 1834, there were still some small Indian villages there. He built his home on the wooded ridges along the north shore after noticing that this was where the Native Americans wintered.

Rogers built just south of the northern Indian Boundary Line, which was the result of an 1816 treaty designating safe passage for whites within a twenty-mile-wide tract of land that ran from Lake Michigan to the Mississippi River, a treaty that was rendered meaningless by the Indian Removal Act of 1830, which dictated that all of the land east of the Mississippi would be open to white settlement. The northern Indian Boundary Line, which was originally an Indian trail, would eventually become Rogers Avenue. And my apartment building would be built on the north corner of Rogers Avenue, just within the former Indian Territory.

During my first weeks in Rogers Park, I was surprised by how often I heard the word "pioneer." I heard it first from the white owner of an antiques shop with signs in the windows that read, "Warning, you are being watched and recorded." When I stopped off in his shop, he welcomed me to the neighborhood warmly and delivered an introductory speech dense with code. This was a "pioneering neighborhood" he told me, and it needed "more people like you." He and other "people like us" were gradually "lifting it up."

And then there was the neighbor across the street, a white man whom my husband met while I was swimming. He told my husband that he had lived here for twenty years, and asked how we liked it. "Oh, we love it," my husband said. "We've been enjoying Clark Street." The tone of the conversation shifted with the mention of Clark Street, our closest shopping street, which is lined with taquerias and Mexican groceries. "Well," the man said, in obvious disapproval, "we're pioneers here."

The word "pioneer" betrays a disturbing willingness to repeat the worst mistake of the pioneers of the American West— the mistake of considering an inhabited place uninhabited. To imagine oneself as a pioneer in a place as densely populated as Chicago is either to deny the existence of your neighbors or to cast them as natives who must be displaced. Either way, it is a hostile fantasy.

My landlord, who grew up in this apartment building, the building his grandfather built, is a tattooed, Harley-riding man who fought in Vietnam and has a string of plastic skulls decorating the entrance to his apartment. When I ask him about the history of this neighborhood, he speaks so evasively that I don't learn anything except that he once felt much safer here than he does now. "We never used to have any of this," he says, gesturing toward the back gate and the newly bricked wall that now protects the courtyard of this building from the alley. "We never even used to lock our doors, even—I used to come home from school and let myself in without a key."

For some time, the front door of the little house that Laura's pa built on the prairie was covered with only a quilt, but when Pa built a door, he designed it so that the latchstring could be pulled in at night and no one could enter the house from outside. Pa padlocked the stable as soon as it was built, and then, after some Indians stopped by and asked Ma to give them her cornmeal, Pa padlocked the cupboards in the kitchen. These padlocks now strike me as quite remarkable, considering that Pa did not even have nails with which to construct the little house but used wooden pegs instead.

In one scene of *Little House*, the house is ringed by howling wolves, in another, a roaring prairie fire sweeps around the house, in another, a panther screams an eerie scream and the girls are kept inside. And then there are the Indians. The Indians who ride by silently, the Indians who occasionally come to the door of the house and ask for food or tobacco, the Indians who are rumored—falsely, as Pa reveals—to have started the prairie fire to drive out the settlers. Toward the end of the book, the Indians hold a "jamboree," singing and chanting all night, so that the family cannot sleep. Pa stays up late making bullets, and Laura wakes to see Pa sitting on a chair by the door with his gun across his knees.

This is our inheritance, for those of us who imagine ourselves pioneers. We don't seem to have retained the frugality of the original pioneers, or their resourcefulness, but we have inherited a ring of wolves around a door covered only by a quilt. And we have inherited padlocks on our pantries. That we carry with us a residue of the pioneer experience is my best explanation for the fact that my white neighbors seem to feel besieged in this neighborhood. Because that feeling cannot be explained by anything else that I know to be true about our lives here.

The adult characters in *Little House,* all of them except for Pa, are fond of saying, "The only good Indian is a dead Indian." And for this reason some people don't want their children reading the book. It is probably true that *Little House* is not, after all, a children's book, but it is a book that does not fail to interrogate racism. And although Laura is guilty of fearing the Indians, she is among the chief interrogators:

> "Why don't you like Indians, Ma?" Laura asked, and
> she caught a drip of molasses with her tongue.

"I just don't like them; and don't lick your fingers,
Laura," said Ma.

"This is Indian country, isn't it?" Laura said. "What
did we come to their country for, if you don't like them?"

With the benefit of sixty years of hindsight, Laura Ingalls
Wilder knew, by the time she wrote *Little House,* that the pioneers who had so feared Native Americans had been afraid of
a people whom they were in the process of nearly exterminat-
ing. And so as a writer she took care, for instance, to point out
that the ribs of the Indians were showing, a reminder that they
came, frighteningly, into the house for food not because they
were thieves but because they were starving. They were starving because the pioneers were killing all their game. If anyone
had a claim on fear, on terror, in the American frontier, it was
obviously the Indians, who could not legally own or buy the
land they lived on and so were gradually being driven out of
their lives.

Near the very end of *Little House,* after the nights of whoop-
ing and chanting that had been terrifying the Ingalls family,
and after many repetitions of the phrase "the only good Indian
is a dead Indian," Pa meets an Indian in the woods, the first
Indian he has met who speaks English, and he learns from him
that the tall Indian who recently came into the house and ate
some food and smoked silently with Pa has saved their lives.
Several tribes came together for a conference and decided to
kill the settlers, but this tall Indian refused, thus destroying a
federation of tribes and saving the settlers. On reporting the
news to his family, Pa declares, "That's one good Indian."

This turn of events has the advantage of offering a lesson and also of being a fairly accurate account of what took place in Kansas in 1869. Because Laura Ingalls Wilder was actually only a toddler during the time her family lived in Kansas, she did quite a bit of research for *Little House,* traveling back to Kansas with her daughter and writing to historians, in the process discovering the story of the tall Indian, Soldat du Chene.

And so Wilder the writer and the researcher knows that the land the Ingallses have made their home on in *Little House* is part of the Osage Diminished Reserve. It is unclear whether Pa knows this, but it is clear that he knows he is in Indian Territory. He goes into Indian Territory on speculation, because he has heard that the government is about to open it up to settlers. At the end of the book, he gets word from his neighbors that the government has decided to uphold its treaty with the Indians and that soldiers will be coming to move the settlers off the land.

"If some blasted politicians in Washington hadn't sent out word it would be all right to settle here, I'd never have been three miles over the line into Indian Territory," Pa admits, in a rare moment of anger and frustration. "But I'll not wait for the soldiers to take us out. We're going now!"

The Ingalls family did indeed leave their home in Kansas under these circumstances. But the possibility the book suggests, by ending where it does, is that in the end the settlers left Indian Territory to the Indians. "It's a great country, Caroline," Pa says as they ride off in their covered wagon. "But there will be wild Indians and wolves here for many a long day."

This is how it could have been, Laura Ingalls Wilder seems

to be proposing. The government could have enforced a fair policy. The settlers could have left and stayed away. But, as it happened, the government revoked its treaty with the Plains tribes within what one historian estimates was a few weeks after the Ingalls family abandoned their house in Kansas.

Laura Ingalls Wilder does not tell us this. She tells us, instead, that Pa digs up the potatoes he just planted and they eat them for dinner. The next day, they get back into their covered wagon, leaving the plow in the field, leaving their new glass windows, leaving their house and their stable, and leaving the crop they have just planted. This is the end of the book, and this, I believe, is the moral of the story.

ON THE LAKE

Walking out of my apartment one morning, I found a piece of paper on the sidewalk that read, "Help! We have no hot water." This message was printed in pink ink above an address that I recognized as being nearby but farther inland from the lake. The paper was carried by the wind to the water's edge, I imagined, as a reminder of the everyday inconveniences, the absent landlords and the delayed buses and the check-cashing fees, of the world beyond.

"Everyone who lives in a neighbourhood belongs to it, is part of it," Geoff Dyer writes in Out of Sheer Rage. "The only way to opt out of a neighbourhood is to move out." But this does not seem to hold true of the thin sliver of Rogers Park bordering the lake, where many of our white neighbors drive in and out and do not walk down Howard to the train station, do not visit the corner store for milk or beer, do not buy vegetables in the little markets, do not, as one neighbor admitted to me, even park farther inland than one block from the lake, no matter how heavily the lakeshore is parked up or how long it takes to find a spot.

Between my apartment building and the lake there is a small park with a stony beach and some cracked tennis courts where people like to let their dogs run loose. In the winter, the only people in the park are people with dogs, people who stand in the tennis courts, holding bags of shit while their dogs run around in circles and sniff one another. In the summer, the park fills with people. Spanish-speaking families make picnics on the grass and Indian families have games of cricket and fathers dip their babies in the lake and groups of black teenagers sit on the benches and young men play volleyball in great clouds of dust until dusk. "The warm weather," my landlord observed to me not long after I moved in, "brings out the riffraff."

When my landlord said this, I was standing on the sidewalk in front of our building in my bathing suit, still dripping from the lake, and a boy leaving the park asked if I had a quarter. I laughed and told the boy that I don't typically carry change in my bathing suit, but he remained blank-faced, as uninterested as a toll collector. His request, I suspect, had very little to do with any money I may have had or any money he may have needed. The exchange was intended to be, like so many of my exchanges with my neighbors, a ritual offering. When I walk from my apartment to the train I am asked for money by all variety of people—old men and young boys and women with babies. Their manner of request is always different, but they are always black and I am always white. Sometimes I give money and sometimes I do not, but I do not feel good about it either way, and the transaction never fails to be complicated. I do not know whether my neighbors think, as I do, of these quarters and dollars as a kind of tax on my presence here. A tax that, although I resent it, is more than fair.

One day in the late summer after we moved to Rogers Park, my husband came home from the fruit market with a bag of tomatoes and a large watermelon, which he had carried the half mile from the market to our house, stopping once to let some children feel how heavy it was. He was flushed from the sun, and as he split the melon, still warm, my husband mused, "I hope more white people don't move here." My husband isn't prone to sentimentality of any kind, or to worrying about white people, so I asked him why, and he said, "Because, kids were playing basketball by the school and they had cheerleaders cheering them on, and black men say hello to me on the street, and I love our little fruit market, and I don't want this place to change."

But this place will probably change, if only because this is not a city where integrated neighborhoods last very long. And we are the people for whom the new coffee shop has opened. And the pet-grooming store. "You know your neighborhood is gentrifying," my sister observes, "when the pet-grooming store arrives." "Gentrification" is a word that agitates my husband. It bothers him because he thinks that the people who tend to use the word negatively, white artists and academics, people like me, are exactly the people who benefit from the process of gentrification. "I think you should define the word 'gentrification,'" my husband tells me now. I ask him what he would say it means, and he pauses for a long moment. "It means that an area is generally improved," he says finally, "but in such a way that everything worthwhile about it is destroyed."

My dictionary defines "gentrify" as meaning "to renovate or improve (esp. a house or district) so that it conforms to middle-class taste." There is definitely the sense among the middle-class people in this neighborhood that they are improving the place. New condos fly banners that read "Luxury!" The coffee shop and pet-grooming store have been billed as a "revitalization." And if some people lose their neighborhood in the process, there is bound to be someone like Mrs. Scott of *Little House* who will say, "Land knows, they'd never do anything with this country themselves. All they do is roam around over it like wild animals. Treaties or no treaties, the land belongs to folks that'll farm it. That's only common sense and justice."

Meanwhile, when I walk home from the train station at night I watch unmarked cars pull in front of black teenagers, who are patted down quickly and wordlessly. Some of the teenagers, my husband observes, carry their IDs in clear cases hanging from their belts for easy access. One evening, I watch the police interrogate two boys who have set a large bottle of Tide down on the sidewalk next to them, and I cannot forget this detail, the bottle of Tide, and the mundane tasks of living that it evokes. I consider going to one of the monthly beat meetings the police hold for each neighborhood and making some kind of complaint, but month after month I do not go.

Walking down Clark Street I pass a poster on an empty storefront inviting entrepreneurs to start businesses in Rogers

Park, "Chicago's most diverse neighborhood." It takes me some time, standing in front of this poster, to understand why the word "diverse" strikes me as so false in this context, so disingenuous. It is not because this neighborhood is not full of many different kinds of people, but because that word implies some easy version of this difficult reality, some version that is not full of sparks and averted eyes and police cars. But still, I'd like to believe in the promise of that word. Not the sunshininess of it, or the quota-making politics of it, but the real complexity of it.

ON THE COAST

There are three of us here on the beach, with Lake Michigan stretching out in front of us. We are strangers, but we have the kind of intimacy that can exist between people who are lying on the same deserted beach. Aisha, a young black woman, sits on one side of me, and Andre, a middle-aged Polish immigrant, sits on the other.

We bury our feet in the sand and talk of the places where we have lived. Aisha is from Chicago, and she has never, in her twenty-one years, lived anywhere else. Andre left Poland when he was seventeen, looking for more opportunities. Now, he says, he isn't entirely sure that he didn't make a mistake. We all fall silent after this confession.

This beach is a kind of no man's land. To the south are the last city blocks of Chicago, where the beaches are free but rocky and plagued with chunks of concrete. To the north are the first city blocks of Evanston, where the beaches are expansive and sandy but require a fee of seven dollars. To the west, beyond the wall of rocks directly behind us, is the cemetery that separates Chicago from Evanston, and the sign that forbids entry to this stretch of beach. To the east is an endless prairie of water.

When I mention that yesterday a lifeguard from Evanston came down in a boat while I was swimming and informed me that it was illegal to be here and that I had to leave because this land belongs to Evanston, Aisha rolls her eyes and says, gesturing back toward the cemetery, "This land belongs to the dead people." Andre looks out across the water and says, "This land belongs to God."

Nobody Knows Your Name

We are driving through Chicago and the radio is screaming "Save me! Somebody save me . . . ," as the bricks of the city pour past us. "Aretha," I suggest. My husband laughs and says, "I'd like a little Aretha." There is a long pause in our conversation while my husband drives and I look out the window. Then he says carefully, "I'm thinking of looking into some Irish names."

My husband's last name is the name of a town in Ireland. He has never been to that town, or to Ireland. Right now we are driving from where we live, on the far north side of Chicago, to where my husband grew up, on the far south side of Chicago. This is a distance of nearly fifty miles, which allows me quite a bit of time to think about what it would mean for us to give our child an Irish name.

The Irish were the first people the English called savages. Like the Native Americans, to whom the English would later compare them, the native people of Ireland were driven from their land. Their villages and crops were burned by the English, and those who were not killed were relocated to reservations. Under the English occupation of Ireland, Irish Catholics were forbidden from, among other things, voting, holding office, teaching, and purchasing land. They were thought of, and thought of themselves, as a distinct race. The English considered them "beasts" naturally given to "idleness" and "sloth." Eighteenth-century Ireland, the historian Noel Ignatiev writes, "presents a classic case of racial oppression."

Despite his interest in Irish names, my husband doesn't tend to think of himself as Irish. When asked, he is much more likely to say that he is white trash. What he means by this is that when he left the South Side, he discovered that other white people lived, invariably, in bigger houses than any he had ever been in, with nicer things, and had better table manners, and didn't talk like he did, and had seen better doctors, and gone to better schools, and knew things he had never learned. In this way, our distinction between "white" and "white trash" is not entirely unlike the distinction between the English and the Irish of the eighteenth century.

My last name is English, and my Polish grandmother, who married into the name, claims I could be a member of the Daughters of the American Revolution. That is all I know of my English heritage. When I was a teenager, I listened to the band Black 47, their name a reference to the worst year of the potato famine. They were Irish expatriates who lived in the Bronx and played rock crossed with reggae, hip-hop, and Irish folk music. My little brother, who was about ten at the time, became fascinated with Black 47. Their lyrics, rich with references to the struggle for Irish independence, would play out for him like puzzles, and after years of memorizing lyrics, he began to read biographies. There was James Connolly, the socialist leader who was tied to a chair and shot after the Easter Rising: "My name is James Connolly—I didn't come here to die, but to fight for the rights of the working man, and the small farmer too." And there was Bobby Sands, the IRA member who starved to death on a hunger strike in jail: "My name is Bobby Sands, MP, born in the city of Belfast, divided by religion, I grew up fast."

And this is how my brother became a student of history.

One of the problems, my brother points out to me now, with comparing the Irish to Native Americans—or African Americans, for that matter—is that England and Ireland had a long history of cultural exchange before Ireland was colonized. And although the Celts of Ireland and the Anglo-Saxons of England are still, even to this day, thought of as two distinct peoples with distinctly different ancestry, scientists have found them to be remarkably similar, genetically speaking, and have suggested that both Britain and Ireland have been populated by a single people for thousands of years. There was, as is usually the case, very little biological basis for the fact that the English regarded the Irish as a separate race in the eighteenth century. This concept was purely social and served a purely social purpose. By the time Ireland was merged with England in 1800, the Irish were the English, and the English were the Irish.

We are driving through the first neighborhoods of the Southeast Side on Stony Island Avenue, past outdoor thrift markets with rows of faded green chairs, liquor stores topped with razor wire, and live bait shops. Shortly after we moved to Chicago, my husband and I looked at a series of maps on which neighborhoods that were more than 90 percent white were colored blue and neighborhoods that were more than 90 percent black were colored red. As we flipped through the maps, one for every ten years of the past century, a red area on the south side budded and then bloomed, and my husband said, with surprise, "My father wasn't crazy!" His father, an Irish Catholic, may have been prejudiced and paranoid, but he was not exactly crazy when he told his son that blacks chased him out of the city. His father moved farther south each time black people began to move into his neighborhood, until eventually he no longer lived in the city or the state.

Whiteness is the distinction many of us cling to when we have nothing else. But poor whites, who were once the primary targets of the eugenics movement—sterilized so that they would not doom their children to poverty and ignorance—have always had more in common with poor blacks than with anyone else. "To the rich white ruling class," the writer Sherman Alexie observes, "working-class whites are actually working-class blacks."

In 1841, sixty thousand Irish nationals signed an address to Irish emigrants in the United States that read, in part:

> America is cursed by slavery! WE CALL UPON
> YOU TO UNITE WITH THE ABOLITIONISTS,
> and never to cease your efforts until perfect liberty be
> granted to every one of her inhabitants, the black man
> as well as the white man. . . . Irishmen and Irishwomen!

Treat the colored people as your equals, as brethren. By
your memories of Ireland, continue to love liberty—
hate slavery—CLING BY THE ABOLITIONISTS—
and *in America you will do honor to the name of Ireland.*

Irish immigrants did not, for the most part, take this plea to
heart. Their social position was too tenuous. They lived among
free blacks in Northern cities and competed for jobs with them.
In the South, they were hired for work that plantation owners
considered too dangerous for slaves. They drained bogs and
died by the hundreds digging canals.

My husband slows the car because we are passing through
Pullman, where an enormous brick factory building still stands,
roofless. Back in 1885, before it became part of Chicago, Pullman
was supposed to be a model town, a town that would be so
clean and comfortable that the factory workers, whose rents
were deducted directly from their paychecks, would never strike.
During the World's Fair it was a tourist attraction, and it was
voted the world's most perfect town in 1896.

Pullman was built for German, English, and Irish workers,
but now most of the people who live here are black. We drive
slowly through the center of the town, past a building with
arches and columns in ruins, and then down a street of beautiful
brick row houses. Despite the fact that I know what happened
here, I am moved by these grand houses, moved by the thought
that they were for working people. But these houses, and their
cost, are what brought down the town. George Pullman's workers struck after he cut wages during a depression but failed to

lower rents. There were riots and fires, and then federal troops were called in and the strike was ended, but Pullman the town, the experiment, had failed. The idea of the model town, the worker's paradise, expired for the moment, and Pullman himself died two years later, so terrified of organized labor that he was buried in a lead-lined casket covered with an inch of asphalt, eight steel rails, and eight feet of concrete.

In New York and Philadelphia and Chicago, Irish immigrants moved, by working for less money, into jobs traditionally held by free blacks. The Irish established themselves in machine shops and docks and factories and railroads and construction sites and then refused, strategically, sometimes violently, to work with blacks. Irish immigrants, first and second generation, became the rank and file and later the leaders of the labor organizations that would win them better pay and better conditions in these jobs and that would exclude black workers. These Irish immigrants not only refused to align themselves with black Americans in solidarity, they locked blacks out of their jobs and neighborhoods. And so, over the course of a hundred or so complicated years, years punctuated with race riots and bloody beatings, the Irish became white. It was, even in the small print of history, an ugly process.

But what is remembered now are the signs, posted in the windows of shops and factories, that read, "Help Wanted: No Irish Need Apply." Tip O'Neill remembered these signs publicly, as did Ted Kennedy, but there is no evidence they ever existed. The historian Richard Jensen has observed that there are no photographs or drawings of these signs, no mentions in newspapers or court records, none have been preserved in archives or museums, and the only people who remember seeing them are Irish Catholics. Being that they are entirely absent from the historical record, it is likely that the memory of these signs is a myth. "A myth of victimization," Jensen calls it, a myth invented by a people who were becoming, as a group, something very different from what they once were.

One summer my brother and I drove across the country together, sleeping in my car and arguing at hot gas stations in the desert. On the highways, we passed the time by reading *King Leopold's Ghost* to each other. This is Adam Hochschild's story of the Belgian Congo, of the forced labor imposed on that colony by the rubber industry, of the conditions that led to the deaths of half the people of the Congo. It is also the story of Roger Casement, the Irish patriot who helped expose those abuses. Casement went on, after his time in the Congo, to investigate the British rubber industry's enslavement of natives in Peru, and then to organize a brigade of Irish prisoners of war to fight against the British in the liberation of Egypt, a project that was aborted shortly before Casement was hanged by the British for treason, and a project that is now used as evidence that Casement was insane.

It is likely, my brother says, that Casement had some problems with his mind, but that doesn't mean he was not a visionary. It was Casement's ability to see beyond national boundaries, to understand that all colonized peoples are involved in the same struggle, that fascinated my brother to begin with, that led him to Casement's biography and then to his diaries. From there, my brother went on to write his thesis about Marcus Garvey, the Jamaican whose vision in America was to "unite all people of African ancestry of the world to one great body to establish a country and absolute government of their own." It took some time for me to fully understand how my brother's study of Irish history led him to a black nationalist, despite the fact that the whole process started because I listened to an Irish band that played reggae.

We are listening to Nina Simone now as we drive south, past crooked wood-sided houses and restaurants with faded photos of food in the windows. "My skin is black," she sings. "What do they call me? My name is Aunt Sarah. My name is Aunt Sarah, Aunt Sarah. My skin is yellow.... What do they call me? My name is Saffronia. My name is Saffronia. My skin is tan.... What do they call me? My name is Sweet Thing. My name is Sweet Thing. My skin is brown.... What do they call me?"

My husband pulls up in front of the first house he ever lived in. His father was, when he lived here, already a drinker. And this neighborhood was, back when my husband was born, entirely white. Now it is entirely black. I fail to notice anything about the house my husband once lived in other than the fact that there is a man in overalls and brown work boots lying face down on the porch. We stare at him from the idling car. One of the man's legs moves and then is still again. We drive on, sobered and silent.

When I introduce myself, I am often asked about my first name. "What is that?" people ask, which is a way of asking, "What are you?" but it took me many years to grasp that and to stop saying my name is Greek, which inevitably led to the clarification that, no, I am not Greek. Now I say my name is Southern, which is truer, in that my name was probably introduced to this country not by Greek immigrants but by Southern gentility, who were enamored of Greek and Latin, and who named their children Aloysius and Ulysses and Eulalia, so that such names became traditional in the South. I am not Southern either, but the South is far closer to where I come from than Greece.

When I was younger I used to tell people—because my father's grandparents came from Poland, and because I ate pierogies and kielbasa on holidays—that I was Polish. But nationality is not genetically encoded, and culturally I am no more Polish than I am African. As an American I am, to be most accurate, a little of both. "All those who have been here and all those who are here now are part of what we are and might become," the activist John Garvey writes in *Race Traitor*. "But, we need to be clear about what we are and what we want to become."

I recently came across an article in *National Geographic* that opened with a two-page photograph of a group of mostly naked women and men dancing in a circle, carrying burning torches. The woman in the center of the frame screamed, openmouthed, directly into the camera, and the photo was very much like the strange photos of black people that I used to examine in *National Geographic* as a child, with the exception that the people in this photo were white. The article was titled "Celt Appeal," and it was about exactly that—the powerful appeal that the remnants of ancient Celtic culture hold for people from outside that culture.

In an already troubled magazine, this article struck me as being particularly oblivious to context. For one, it acknowledged a widespread fascination with Celtic culture without discussing what might be motivating so many people whose lives do not remotely resemble the lives of ancient Celts to identify with that culture. "'Europe's beautiful losers,' as one British writer called them, are commanding attention as one of the new century's seductive identities: free-spirited, rebellious, poetic, nature-worshipping, magical, self-sufficient," the author, Tom O'Neill, writes, but he does not seem to feel the need to explain the new century's shopping spree for identities, particularly white identities that have remained untainted by colonialism. O'Neill, an American, does make it clear that our identities are ours to choose. "There are 'blood Celts,'" he writes, "the several million people who were raised and still live in the surviving Celtic language territories. Then there is the growing tribe of 'Celts of the spirit,' who feel touched by the history, myths, and artistic expressions of beautiful losers." Later in the article he interviews a Cornish goddess worshipper who says, "I believe if you feel Celtic, you become Celtic."

There is something disingenuous about European Americans—particularly those whom it might be fair to call the "winners," in terms of economic power and freedom in America—adopting the identity of Europe's "losers" because we recognize belatedly how much we lost in the transaction that made us white in this country. Perhaps seeing ourselves as descendants, in blood or in spirit, of historically oppressed peoples is an important step toward aligning ourselves with our brethren in this country. But if we want a people to identify with, we have our own beautiful losers. And we have their culture already—we live within it. We have blues and jazz and hip-hop, and we have the food and sports and dances and clothing styles made unique to America by black Americans. White suburban teenagers know this, and some of them embrace black culture for that brief moment in which they are powerless in the land of the powerful. But what keeps so many of the rest of us, as adults, from deliberately identifying with our own beautiful losers? Perhaps we are reluctant to discover what that would require of us. And we don't have anyone telling us, "I believe if you feel black, you become black."

On our way into the neighborhood where my husband spent most of his childhood we pass a billboard that reads "I SEE BLACK PEOPLE" in big block letters, and we laugh in surprise because we do, indeed, see black people. We turn off the main strip, with its diners and video rentals and signs for cocktails, and then we turn off again, and now we are driving through rows of little one-story houses lined up neatly on small patches of grass. This is Calumet City, on the far south side of Chicago's far south side. And this was, when my husband was young, the place where the men who worked in the factories on Lake Michigan lived. Most of those factories have left, or closed, and my husband wonders aloud where the people who live here work now.

He wants to drive me into the adjoining neighborhood to show me the contrast between this modest neighborhood, with its cramped alleys and the much wealthier one next door, but he becomes confused when we drive down a street that unexpectedly dead-ends. And then he circles back around, only to find that a fence blocks us from entering the road we need to cross to reach the rich neighborhood. That neighborhood happens to be on the other side of the Indiana state line, and now we discover that there is a short concrete median on State Line Avenue running the length of that border. We can't go over there. My husband is puzzled and distressed. He thinks his memory is failing him. He keeps saying, "It wasn't like this before." Finally, he gives up, saying, "I guess they decided to keep the black people out."

There is, I've discovered, no town with my husband's last name on the map of Ireland. None of the six other spellings of his name are there either. His name appears on marriage records and gravestones and lists of laborers from Ireland, but it is not on the map, and he does not now remember why he thought it was. If it ever existed, the place that gave my husband his name is gone, and the name, in its many incarnations, its many variations, its many pronunciations, is all that is left of that place.

My children, when I have them, will take my husband's name. And that name, by the time it reaches them, will be no more Irish than it is American. I know nothing about these future children other than that they will be white, but my hope for them is that their lives will change the meaning of that distinction. Perhaps I will tell them that your race is like your name—it is a given, and you must define your own name so that it does not define you. How will I explain what I mean by this? I'll play Nina Simone, who, in that chilling moment of song, that blistering redefinition of everything she has ever been called, tells us, "My . . . name . . . is . . . Peaches!"

After

All Apologies

When we were young, my best friend's older brother taught him the first rule of catch—don't apologize. Especially if you drop the ball or overthrow.

The year I turned eleven, Reagan signed legislation officially apologizing for the internment of Japanese Americans during World War II. He had originally threatened to veto the measure because of its cost.

My sister stood in the doorway with her tiny arms stretched out to grip the doorjamb, smiling. Her ladybug T-shirt didn't quite cover her little round tummy. And that's where I punched her. There was no hesitation, no moment of doubt. She was standing there with her arms out and I punched her stomach. It was an experiment. And I was sorry the instant my fist hit her. Sorry even before I saw her face, covered in shock, a horrible purple. I had knocked the wind out of her toddler's body, and she was rolling around on the floor. "I'm sorry," I gasped. "I'm sorry." But already I felt something else. I grabbed her arm desperately. "Please," I said, "don't tell."

The men who killed children in the village of No Gun Ri during the Korean War did not tell until they were asked. Some still did not tell. The officer who had given or not given the orders was dead. One veteran, Ed Daily, said that he was haunted by the sound of little kids screaming. He confessed to participating in the atrocity and helped the press investigate the role of his unit, the Seventh Cavalry Regiment. At a ceremony in Cleveland, Ed Daily embraced a survivor of the massacre.

On the day he signed the bill apologizing to Japanese Americans, Reagan resisted apology. "It's not for us today to pass judgment upon those who may have made mistakes while engaged in that great struggle," he said. "Yet we must recognize that the internment of Japanese Americans was just that, a mistake."

As adults, my siblings begin to remember some of the crimes of childhood as accidents. My sister no longer claims that the scar on her face is my fault.

In the same year that Japan's parliament was debating a resolution to apologize for its role in World War II, George H. W. Bush refused the suggestion that he should apologize for the

atomic bombs dropped on Hiroshima and Nagasaki. He called
the idea of apologizing for the bombs "rank revisionism."

In the basement, with the beekeeping equipment and the vat
full of honey, my littlest sister first said the phrase that would
plague my childhood: "Sorry doesn't cut it." I was baffled. My
sister would no longer, as a matter of policy, accept my apologies.
The words "sorry doesn't cut it" appeared again and again—
after each insult, each scratch, each slap. What followed an apology from then on was an enraging reminder that every action is
essentially irrevocable.

Youth, you might think, is one thing we do not owe an apology for. But I am certain there are ways of being young that are
unforgivable.

The year I turned twenty, Congress proposed a bill officially
apologizing for slavery. Jesse Jackson called it "meaningless,"
and Newt Gingrich, "a dead end."

"For a serious offense," writes psychiatrist Aaron Lazare, "such
as a betrayal of trust or public humiliation, an immediate apology misses the mark. It demeans the event. Hours, days, weeks,
or even months may go by before both parties can integrate the
meaning of the event and its impact on the relationship. The
care and thought that goes into such apologies dignifies the exchange. For offenses whose impact is calamitous to individuals, groups, or nations, the apology may be delayed by decades
and offered by another generation."

While the country debated whether Clinton should issue an apology for slavery, a member of the Cayuga Nation called for him to apologize to the Native Americans.

The historic Seventh Cavalry Regiment was the unit that opened fire on Indian women and children at Wounded Knee Creek. Ed Daily joined the Seventh Cavalry more than half a century after Wounded Knee. In 1993 he attended a peace ceremony in South Dakota with members of the Lakota Sioux tribe, and then in 1999 he attended a prayer service in Cleveland for victims of the massacre at No Gun Ri.

Ed Daily was not at Wounded Knee, of course, but army documents show that Ed Daily was not actually at No Gun Ri either. He spent most of the war as a mechanic and a clerk behind the front lines, and he joined the Seventh Cavalry Regiment eight months after the massacre at No Gun Ri. He confessed to an atrocity he did not commit. At the ceremony in Cleveland, Daily said that he was "very sympathetic with the survivors and what they've endured." He came closer to apologizing than any of the soldiers who actually fired on civilians.

Some apologies are unspeakable. Like the one we owe our parents.

"Daily has this thing about apologizing," said a former Seventh Cavalry officer. Ed Daily's memories of the war began to emerge after his marriage ended. He had never spoken of the war to his wife.

During his first campaign, Clinton apologized for "wrong-doing" in his marriage. Within a year of his election, he formally apologized to Hawaiians for the overthrow of Queen Liliuokalani a century before. In his second term, Clinton apologized on behalf of the federal government for an experiment conducted from 1932 to 1972 in which hundreds of black men had been denied treatment for syphilis and allowed to die.

My friend taught me the first rule of catch not because we were playing catch, but because I had a habit of apologizing too much.

Women apologize as often to their friends as to strangers. Men rarely apologize to their friends. "Men," the linguist Janet Holmes writes, "seem to avoid apologies where possible."

President Clinton referred the question of whether or not he should apologize for slavery to an advisory group. It was decided that he should not apologize.

I waited for almost an entire day to see a doctor in a Brooklyn clinic packed with fifty women without health insurance. Those of us who were not pregnant stood so that the others could sit. I was the only white woman in the room. The doctor who examined me, finally, was a very quiet, gentle man. When he lifted the paper blanket that covered my legs, he said softly, "I'm sorry." He pushed my knees apart, saying twice, "I'm sorry." The nurse handed him something. "I'm sorry, does this hurt?" he asked. "I'm sorry," he said, pressing down on my stomach with two fingers. He hesitated. "I'm sorry, miss, I need to lift your shirt." He examined my breasts, saying, "I'm sorry. . . ."

Some of us learn as children that it is often better to apologize for something we did not do than to try to maintain our innocence. And some of us do not learn this until we are adults.

I walked home from the clinic in Brooklyn grateful to have finally received an apology for the vulnerability of my body. An apology from a man. The doctor's apologies were important— necessary, even. And he was guilty of nothing.

While in Africa, Clinton expressed his regret for U.S. participation in slavery, for U.S. support of dictators during the cold war, for U.S. neglect and ignorance of Africa, for the failure of the United States to intervene in the Rwandan genocide, and for U.S. complicity in apartheid.

F. W. de Klerk apologized for apartheid.

Nelson Mandela apologized for atrocities committed by the African National Congress in fighting against apartheid.

Mathieu Kérékou, president of Benin, apologized on his knees in Baltimore for the African role in the slave trade.

President Johannes Rau said, "I pay tribute to all those who were subjected to slave and forced labor under German rule, and, in the name of Germany, beg forgiveness."

In Uganda, Clinton departed from his prepared text to say, "Going back to the time before we were a nation, European Americans received the fruits of the slave trade, and we were wrong in that."

"Stop," my brother told me. We were standing in the yard with rakes in our hands. My little brother was not a skinny kid anymore. He was fully grown, and we stood facing each other suddenly as adults. "You always do that," he told me, "and then you think you can just apologize. If you were really sorry, you wouldn't do it again."

After publishing a report in 2000 on how Aetna Insurance had profited from slavery, the *Hartford Courant* apologized for having accepted advertisements for slaves. Aetna then officially apologized for having insured slaves as property.

An apology is also an admission of guilt. Public apologies can have legal consequences. And a cost: $1.25 billion for the survivors of the Japanese American internment camps, $10 million for the victims of the Tuskegee syphilis experiment, $5.1 billion for forced laborers under the Nazi regime . . .

Aetna was among a series of insurance, railroad, tobacco, and financial firms recently sued for profiting from slavery. The plaintiffs in one case asked that the companies establish a fund for the health care, housing, and education of African Americans.

What is an apology without forty acres and a mule?

Clinton chose his language very carefully. About Rwanda, he said that, at the time, he "did not fully appreciate" the extent of the genocide. Not that he did not know. Because he did know. The *Washington Post* reported piles of bodies six feet high, and the evening news showed rivers choked with corpses. Regret, not action, had been his policy decision. Regret, he hoped, would not cost him anything.

Clinton settled with Paula Jones for $850,000 after telling her to "kiss it." She said she wasn't sorry she didn't get him to apologize.

A boy hissed at me in the hall while I was on my way to the bathroom. As I spun around, angry, I realized that he might have thought I was another student. "Watch yourself," I said, "I'm a teacher." He gave me a low-lidded half smile and looked me up and down. A kid—he was a kid in a baseball cap. But he was a foot taller than me and he leaned in to say, "Mmmm, so wuz your name?" Then I sat in the office of the Harlem school, sorry I had said anything, while my boss went to hunt down the kid. I had the sickening sense that I was about to be responsible for a lynching on my own tiny plantation. A boy came to the door of the office and looked at me uncertainly. "I'm sorry I sexually harassed you." I stared at him. He wasn't the same kid. "But it wasn't you," I said finally. "Yeah," he said as he pulled down his baseball cap and started to walk away, "but it might have been my cousin."

Like me, my cousins have European blood. They also have the colonized blood of Jamaica and the massacred blood of Native

Americans. My skin is white, but I still have the ravaged blood of Africa in me.

The most necessary apology is the apology for what we have done to ourselves.

More than one hundred years after the first antilynching bill was proposed by a black congressman, the United States Senate voted to apologize for failing to ban lynching during the twentieth century. "There may be no other injustice in American history," Senator Mary Landrieu said, "for which the Senate so uniquely bears responsibility." The resolution to apologize was passed in the presence of a cousin of Emmett Till, a teenager who was lynched for whistling at a white woman.

Monica Lewinsky told Barbara Walters that she had waited a long time to tell the country she was sorry.

"In general, women apologised more than men for intrusions on the space of another person," writes Janet Holmes of a study on patterns of apology. "They were more likely than men to apologise for bumping into another person, for instance. In fact when women bumped into each other, both generally said *sorry*. It is perhaps not surprising to find a predominance of apologies for accidental body contact in a group who are the main victims of sexual harassment."

Clinton expressed regret. Clinton then expressed profound regret. Finally, Clinton said he was "very sorry" about his relationship with Monica Lewinsky.

"I regret our long neglect of the planet Pluto. It took until 1930 to welcome Pluto into the family of planets. And that was wrong," Clinton said to laughter at a 1998 dinner. "And I am so sorry . . . about disco."

Monica Lewinsky noted that the president had apologized to everyone except her. "I think he's sorry he got caught," she said.

Clinton's regret over Rwanda did not move George W. Bush. "I don't like genocide," Bush said during his campaign for presidency. "But I would not commit our troops."

During George W. Bush's first year in office, the Chinese government requested a formal apology from the United States after an American spy plane collided with a Chinese fighter plane, killing the pilot of the fighter plane and making an unauthorized emergency landing in China. Bush refused the request and China held the crew of the plane. After a week of stalemate, Colin Powell was the first to publicly use the words "sorrow" and "sorry." The Bush administration finally issued a letter saying that the United States was "sorry" about the death of the Chinese pilot.

I broke a flowerpot in Mexico. *"Lo siento, lo siento, lo siento,"* I kept repeating to a woman who only stared at me. Were these the right words? I was sure they were, but the woman said nothing. An apology is incomplete until it is accepted.

If I apologized for slavery, would you accept?

The Chinese government rejected the first draft of the letter of regret offered by the United States and asked for a stronger apology. The Bush administration revised the letter to say that the United States was "very sorry" about the death of the pilot.

There are several words for apology in Chinese. One can simply acknowledge a loss, one can excuse a mistake without taking responsibility, or one can admit guilt and express remorse.

The final letter of U.S. regret was issued only in English, which allowed the term "very sorry" to be translated by the Chinese as *dao qian,* which implies that the speaker admits wrongdoing. After the letter was accepted, Colin Powell said that the United States had nothing to apologize for. "He landed without permission," Powell said of the American pilot, "and we're very sorry—but we're glad he did."

Near the end of his first term, the State Department recommended that Bush apologize for the abuses in the Abu Ghraib prison. When Bush did not apologize in his interviews with two Arab television channels, the king of Jordan suggested that if the president wanted to begin to calm outrage over the scandal, he should apologize.

The year I turned thirty, I wrote to the friend who taught me the first rule of catch and apologized for being young once. My friend did not respond.

"Given the president's simultaneous and reiterated insistence that neither he nor his staff have done anything wrong and that there is nothing to change in his policies or goals, who will take seriously such an apology, extracted in extremis?" asked NYU professor Tony Judt of the proposed apology for Abu Ghraib. "Like confessions obtained under torture, it is worthless."

My childhood might have been different if I had known that it is possible to apologize without apologizing. I might have been spared the pain of learning.

"I told him," Bush said to reporters after his conversation with King Abdullah, "I was sorry for the humiliation suffered by the Iraqi prisoners, and the humiliation suffered by their families. I told him I was equally sorry that people who have been seeing those pictures didn't understand the true nature and heart of America. . . . I also made it clear to His Majesty that the troops we have in Iraq . . . represent the very best qualities of America— courage, love of freedom, compassion, and decency."

There is only one word for apology in English, but there are several words for a loss of freedom—"internment," "imprison- ment," "detention," "slavery." . . .

Lo siento, meaning, literally, "I feel it."

The United States and Israel walked out of the 2001 World Conference against Racism. Spain issued a statement of "deep regret" over slavery. England did not apologize, for legal reasons. The German foreign minister did not apologize, but he said that recognizing historical guilt could restore "dignity that had been stolen." The French parliament unanimously acknowledged that "the transatlantic and Indian Ocean slave trade, perpetrated from the fifteenth century against Africans, Amerindians, Malagasies and Indians, constitutes a crime against humanity."

I apologize for slavery. It wasn't me, true. But it might have been my cousin.

Notes

ON THE TITLE

The term "no man's land," meaning "debatable land," often served in its earliest usage as the name for a place on or between boundaries. It was later used to mean "an indeterminate state, a state of confusion or uncertainty."

I first remember hearing the term "no man's land" when I was twelve and the Berlin wall had just come down. In order that we might better appreciate the significance of this event, my German teacher tried to explain how profoundly the wall had altered life in Berlin. Having been blessed with a fenceless childhood, I didn't understand how a wall could divide a city, and I wanted to know why people didn't just climb over it, or tunnel under it, or go around it. Some did, my teacher admitted, but the wall was surrounded by a hundred-yard stretch of gravel, and anyone who entered that no man's land would be shot or arrested. What I learned from this lesson, right or wrong, was that it was not so much the wall that divided the city as it was the no man's land around that wall.

ON "TIME AND DISTANCE OVERCOME"

I began my research for this essay by searching for every instance of the phrase "telephone pole" in the *New York Times*
from 1880 to 1920, which resulted in 370 articles. I was plan-
ning to write an essay about telephone poles and telephones,
not lynchings, but after reading an article headlined "Colored
Scoundrel Lynched," and then another headlined "Mississippi
Negro Lynched," and then another headlined "Texas Negro
Lynched," I searched for every instance of the word "lynched"
in the *New York Times* from 1880 to 1920, which resulted in
2,354 articles.

I refer, in this essay, to the first scholar of lynching, meaning
James E. Cutler, author of the 1905 book *Lynch-Law*, in which
he writes, on the first page, "Lynching is a criminal practice
which is peculiar to the United States." This is debatable, of
course, and very possibly not true, but there is good evidence
that the Italian Antonio Meucci invented a telephone years
before Bell began working on his device, so as long as we are
going to lay claim to one invention, we might as well take responsibility for the other.

Bell would say, late in his life: "Recognition for my work
with the deaf has always been more pleasing than the recognition of my work with the telephone." His own hearing was failing by the time he placed the first cross-country call, from New
York to his old friend Thomas Watson in San Francisco, and
what he said to Watson then was an echo of the first sentence
he ever spoke into his invention, a famous and possibly mythi-
cal sentence that is now remembered in several slightly differ-

ent versions, one being, "Mr. Watson, come here—I want you," and another being, "Mr. Watson, come here—I need you!"

ON "RELATIONS"

The degree to which race is unrelated to biology can be difficult to grasp, perhaps because it seems so bound to blood. Professor of biological anthropology Alan Goodman says, "To understand why the idea of race is a biological myth requires a major paradigm shift—an absolute paradigm shift, a shift in perspective. And for me, it's like seeing what it must have been like to understand that the world isn't flat—the world looks flat to our eyes." In a 2003 interview with PBS, Goodman goes on to explain that there is no meaningful grouping of traits within races. For the concept of race to have biological significance, skin color needs to reflect something deeper in the body—but it does not. "There is no there there," Goodman says of race. And our popular racial categories are too fluid to function as scientific categories: "What's black in the United States is not what's black in Brazil or what's black in South Africa. What was black in 1940 is different from what is black in 2000.... Science is based on generalizability, it's based on consistency, it's based on reproducibility. If you have none of that, you have junk science."

The 2005 study of toy brands referenced in this essay—the study that revealed the intense hatred many girls harbor for their Barbie dolls—was conducted at the University of Bath. Some of the ideas in this essay were originally inspired by the work of Noel Ignatiev, author of *How the Irish Became*

White and editor, with John Garvey, of the journal *Race Traitor* ("Treason to whiteness is loyalty to humanity"). Noel Ignatiev was the first person to suggest to me that John Brown was not a lunatic, and he was the first editor to publish my writing. I owe him these debts and many others.

Race Traitor sits on my bookshelf next to *The Women* by Hilton Als. "Negress," Hilton Als writes, is what his mother, a black woman from Barbados, called herself. Als turns this term "Negress" over and over, applying it first to his mother, then to Malcolm X's mother, then to the Harvard-educated Dorothy Dean, and finally to his former lover Owen Dodson. Als thought of himself as a Negress for years. "And yet," he writes, "I have come no closer to defining it."

One of my students, in a valiant effort to understand the shifting meaning of "Negress" as Als uses the term, made a chart in which she arranged all the shared characteristics of his Negresses: a tendency toward protracted suicide or self-destruction, an attraction to the wrong men, a willful romanticism, a slow physical dissolution, and an enduring desire to be saved by love. Faced with this evidence, and willing for the moment to accept a rather simplistic reduction of a complicated book, I realized that my own mother was a Negress. (This no longer strikes me as particularly true, but at the moment it seemed so clear and obvious that I wondered why the thought hadn't occurred to me sooner.) When I suggested this possibility to my students (inspired by Als's willingness to think of Negressity as a quality not necessarily restricted to a particular gender—and so perhaps not restricted to a particular race), one of my students, a white woman, was outraged. I cannot dismiss her outrage entirely, but I also cannot accept that variety of outrage—the kind that forbids us from seeing ourselves in one another—as one I am willing to live by. Als writes: "To women who are not Negresses—some are white—the Negress, whether she calls herself that or not, is a specter of dignity—selfless to a fault. But eventually the Negress troubles her noncolored female admirer, since the latter feels compelled to compare her privilege to what the Negress does not have—recognizable privilege—and finds herself lacking. This inversion or competitiveness among women vis-à-vis their 'oppressed' stance says something about why friendships among women are rare, let alone why friendships between noncolored women and Negresses are especially so."

This essay is for Nadine, with love.

ON "THREE SONGS OF SALVAGE"

In the sixties, during the movement to reclaim an African identity, some African Americans in New York City adopted the Yoruba tradition, a West African religion that first traveled to the New World with slaves. The religion was already practiced in New York by Cuban musicians (it has many cousins, including Santeria in Cuba, Candomblé in Brazil, and Vodou in Haiti), and it eventually found its way to rural upstate New York, where it was practiced by Puerto Ricans and Native Americans and the European Americans of my family. I was about twelve or thirteen when my mother began to take us to *bembé*s. The songs we sang there were in an African language none of us spoke. But these songs had survived generations of being sung by people who didn't understand the words.

While the ritual words had remained the same, the Yoruba tradition had changed around them. In the New World, slaves who had been taken from many different villages—each dedicated to a single orisha—began to worship numerous orishas in one place. And in Cuba many rituals were altered by slaves to be more easily disguised as Catholicism. Santeria, my mother once told me, is the Yoruba tradition translated through the Catholic religion. In the process, it took on elements it did not have before, such as the concept of guilt.

I now live at some distance from my mother's religion. Most of what I know, I've read. The prayers and songs and translations that I quote in this essay are all from John Mason's book *Orin Orisa: Songs for Selected Heads.* Yoruba theology, Mason writes, is embedded in the songs and dances and in the drumbeats themselves.

ON "LAND MINES"

I come from a family of teachers—my brother teaches, my sister teaches, many of my cousins teach, several of my aunts teach, and my grandmother used to teach. When I moved to New York, the teachers I worked with there served as a kind of extended family for me, and I remember their generosity now with tremendous gratitude. If this essay fails to dwell on the love and integrity with which most teachers approach their work, that is only because this strikes me as already obvious.

Most of the information in this essay is based on a research paper I wrote many years ago for a course on Southern history. (My sources included *Schooling for the New Slavery* by Donald Spivey, *Northern Schools, Southern Blacks, and Reconstruction* by Ronald Butchart, *A Union Officer in the Reconstruction* by John De Forest, *Education in American History,* edited by Michael Katz, *A History of Negro Education in the South* by Henry Bullock, and *Reading, 'Riting, and Reconstruction* by Robert Morris.) I can barely stand to read that paper now, but the research I did for it haunted my early years as a teacher. I wrote the first draft of this essay during those years, and I've revised it many times since then, but I haven't managed to revise out the sensibility of the idealistic, indignant, impudent young teacher who first wrote it. That might be because I am still that young teacher. But I tended to think in broader sweeps then, and I had a greater capacity for overstatement. "Sometimes it seems," the writer Marilynne Robinson says, "as if one's own earlier self is a stranger to whom one is also indebted."

ON "GOODBYE TO ALL THAT"

Joan Didion borrowed the title of her 1967 essay "Goodbye to All That" from Robert Graves's 1929 World War I memoir *Goodbye to All That.* I borrowed the title of this essay from Didion, and I also borrowed a few of her sentences. For the most part, I took only her sentence structures, changing the words. But at times I took both the words and the structure, changing only the meaning. For instance, in her essay Didion writes: "Nothing was irrevocable; everything was within reach." And in mine I write: "Everything was irrevocable, and nothing was within reach."

Joan Didion once mentioned in an interview that she taught herself to type by copying over Hemingway's stories. I began copying Didion's "Goodbye to All That" shortly after I left New York for California. But Didion's experience of being young in New York was so different from mine that I found I could not rewrite her essay without changing the words. So this essay began as an exercise and became instead a kind of conversation with Didion about New York and, more important, that other subject Didion has attacked so relentlessly for nearly fifty years—the stories we tell ourselves.

ON "BLACK NEWS"

In support of its statement that "race is the most consistent factor contributing to the decision to remove children and place them in foster care," the National Association of Black Social Workers cites Sheryl Brissett-Chapman's 1997 article "Child Protection Risk Assessment and African American Children: Cultural Ramifications for Families and Communities" and Ashok Chand's 2000 article "The Over-Representation of Black Children in the Child Protection System: Possible Causes, Consequences, and Solutions," among other publications.

The NABSW also notes, in its position paper on kinship care, that "informal adoption, or the rearing of children by relatives, is one of the most enduring African traditions that survived the Middle Passage." It goes on to point out that our current legislation around adoption and foster care often fails to embrace an expansive definition of family. In the African American community, the NABSW explains, family is not limited to people who live within the same household but includes the full range of blood kin, cousins of every degree, relationships through informal marriage, half-siblings, stepsiblings, stepparents, and a broad range of "fictive kin"—godparents, friends, and neighbors.

I don't know whether Ms. Johnson ever won custody of her grandchildren, and I can't bring myself to contact her for the sole purpose of satisfying my curiosity, or yours. If this essay allows for Ms. Johnson to be interpreted as a victim, I'd like to clarify now that I don't believe she was. She was a woman whose mission was much greater than her resources. A woman of ambition. But I don't doubt that her story was more complicated than that too, and more complicated than what I've written.

ON "LETTER TO MEXICO"

The ten-year reports on NAFTA that I reviewed in my research for this essay reflected a variety of conclusions, ranging from muted optimism to mitigated alarm. I drew most of my information from a 2003 study by the Carnegie Endowment for International Peace titled "NAFTA's Promise and Reality: Lessons from Mexico for the Hemisphere," which concluded that NAFTA had failed to generate job growth in Mexico, had hurt subsistence farmers in Mexico, and had failed to stem Mexican emigration to the United States. The study also noted a trend of lower wages in Mexico, despite increased productivity, and an increase in income inequality across Mexico.

Recognizing the reasons you are hated does not, of course,

necessitate hating yourself. But it can give you the blues. In a 2006 lecture titled "The Gifts of Black Folk in the Age of Terrorism," Cornel West observed that 9/11 created an atmosphere in which the entire country could, for the first time, experience the sensation of feeling "unsafe, unprotected, subject to random violence, and hated for who they are." And so the aftermath of 9/11 produced what West called "the niggerization of the nation." Because "to be a nigger in America for the first 350 years is to be unsafe, unprotected, subject to random violence, and hated for who you are." Now all of America, West said, has the blues. And in this moment we might learn from the legacy of our own blues people. In West's words, that means engaging in Socratic self-examination, asking what it means to be human, and wrestling with death in its various forms.

This essay is for Ben, my traveling companion.

ON "BABYLON"

The first chapter of George Lipsitz's *Possessive Investment in Whiteness: How White People Profit from Identity Politics* explores the ways in which a number of twentieth-century laws and policies have benefited whites exclusively, despite the fact that the laws contain no overt racial provisions. To paraphrase Lipsitz's well-documented discussion of housing policies: After World War II, the Federal Housing Administration and private lenders helped create today's segregation by channeling home-loan money away from the inner city and toward the suburbs. Because of racially biased categories in the FHA city surveys and appraisers' manuals, almost all of the FHA loan money went to white home owners. The 1968 Housing and Urban Development Act could have addressed some of the problems with how FHA loans were distributed but was instead used by real-estate agents and speculators to create inflated sales and mortgage foreclosures that profited lenders and destroyed the value of inner-city housing for generations to come by making much of it ineligible for future loans. Between the 1930s and the 1970s, urban renewal programs demolished 1,600 black neighborhoods, and 90 percent of the low-income units destroyed for urban renewal were never replaced. Between 1934 and 1962 the FHA and the Veterans Administration financed more than $120 billlion worth of new housing, but only 2 percent of this went to nonwhite families.

In the 1960s, many white suburban communities gained access to federal funds for "urban aid" by incorporating themselves as municipalities. In the 1970s and 1980s, lenders refused to obey new fair housing laws, and the Federal Home Loan Bank Board redlined areas with increasing minority populations. The 1975 Home Mortgage Disclosure Act and the 1977 Community Reinvestment Act were ignored by the Reagan administration. Now, whites who became home owners under discriminatory circumstances are profiting from the appreciation of their homes. "The appreciated value of owner-occupied homes," writes George Lipsitz, "constitutes the single greatest source of wealth for white Americans. It is the factor most responsible for the disparity between blacks and whites in respect to wealth—a disparity between the two groups much greater than their differences in income. It is the basis of intergenerational transfers of wealth that enable white parents to give their children financial advantages over the children of other groups."

In my research for this essay, I stumbled across a debate over the word *reconquista* on a Wikipedia page of disputed neutrality. The wiki writers seemed to agree that the term was "originally a jocular analogy to the Spanish Reconquista of Moorish Iberia" used "to describe the demographic and cultural reemergence of Mexicans in the Southwestern United States," but they could not agree on whether an activist movement to reclaim the land of the Southwest for people of Mexican descent was real or a right-wing conspiracy theory. On the talk page where the wiki writers argued their points about the main article, several writers noted that the word *reconquista* tends to be used most often by white nativist groups rather than Chicano nationalist groups, and an exploration of the Web pages of a handful of these groups supports this observation.

The adoption of a Spanish term by American nativist groups is interesting, as is the apparent eagerness of those who favor the term *reconquista* to attribute it to indigenous-rights groups like the Mexica Movement. The Mexica Movement, which has engaged in "warrior actions" such as boycotting Disney, does not, as far as I can tell, use the word *reconquista* or the word "reconquest" or the word "conquest" in any of their policy statements. They far prefer the word "liberation." And although they've been accused of "advocating genocide," among other things, their policy statements say that they "want the problem of colonialism solved with a democratic, constitutional, and non-violent solution" and that they "don't want to behave in the savage manner of Europeans." This, of course, is our fear. "Liberation" is translated as "conquest" out of a consuming fear that what our ancestors did to others will be done to us.

This essay owes its inspiration to Psalm 137 (as sung by the Melodians), and much of its information about Oakland as well as some of its metaphors to Robert Self's *American Babylon: Race and the Struggle for Postwar Oakland*.

ON "BACK TO BUXTON"

In a 2007 lecture at Amherst College, Marilynne Robinson spoke about the history of the many small colleges scattered across the Midwest: "They were founded as stations on the underground railway, and as centers for humane learning of a kind that would make their graduates and those influenced by them resistant to the spread of slavery." These colleges were born from the Second Great Awakening and their faculties were drawn from divinity schools. Many of these colleges were racially integrated before the Civil War, but in the twentieth century these same institutions became resistant to integration. "A great amnesia had settled over the whole society," Robinson says of this past century, "a forgetfulness that there had been racially integrated towns with black mayors, even that there had been regiments of black soldiers in the Civil War. It is not only interesting but truly ominous that such a significant part of our history could just slide into eclipse. This is another thing I learned from moving to Iowa, and could have learned in Kansas and virtually anywhere else in the Middle West — that a society with a history full of hope and intention can forget that anything bold or generous, anything of interest, had ever happened there."

The Iowa Women's Archives at the University of Iowa Library helped me in my research for this essay, particularly by pointing me toward the book *Buxton: A Black Utopia in the Heartland* by Dorothy Schwieder, Joseph Hraba, and Elmer Schwieder (this is an updated edition of their 1987 *Buxton: Work and Racial Equality in a Coal Mining Community*). In my multiple readings of this book I occasionally found myself suspicious of the authors' optimism, but I still remain more or less in thrall to that optimism.

A 1948 economic survey by the Industrial and Human Relations Club of St. Ambrose College suggests that the residents of Cook's Point were not forced into their living conditions purely by economic necessity. Housing discrimination almost certainly played a greater role than poverty in building that community. (A former Cook's Point resident who moved to the city of Davenport and bought a home said, "I must be extra careful and work twice as hard with the upkeep of this home because all the people in the neighborhood had their eyes fixed on me.") A 1978 article in the *Quad City Times* notes that former residents of Cook's Point were still holding reunions nearly thirty years after the town was bulldozed, and the photo caption reads, "Although they had no conveniences, residents of Cook's Point held affection for the area. Some had to be forcibly evicted."

ON "IS THIS KANSAS"

My experiment in this essay was to think about students in the way other minority groups are commonly regarded—as a ho-

mogenous, potentially dangerous, downtrodden and victimized, but nevertheless threatening element. An inversion of an
incorrect attitude isn't, of course, a correction of that attitude—
but it can serve as provocation to thought. And I hope for this
essay to be understood as a provocation.

In Karyn McKinney's 2005 book *Being White: Stories of
Race and Racism,* a study of how white college students think
about being white, she found that white students tend to be
blind to any advantages their race might afford them and to feel
that they are actually socially and economically disadvantaged
by their race. This conviction, supported mainly by a poor
understanding of affirmative-action policies, is accompanied
by a belief that racism no longer exists and that whites are now
the primary victims of racial discrimination. These fictions,
McKinney explains, are part of the experience of being white
today. For this reason, she does not judge individual students
on the opinions they express. "I am instead dismayed by the
culture that produces the ideologies reflected there," she writes.
At the University of Iowa, the attitudes of most of my students
echoed the attitudes of the students in McKinney's study, but I
worked with a number of students who resisted these attitudes
or were at least troubled by them. Those students were immersed in a culture that was not serving their minds well, and
this essay is for them.

Slavoj Žižek's essay "The Subject Supposed to Loot and
Rape: Reality and Fantasy in New Orleans" helped me to articulate why I found even the most accurate reporting on Katrina
disturbing. The nuances of his argument are best put in his
words:

Jacques Lacan claimed that, even if the patient's wife is really sleeping around with other men, the patient's jealousy is still to be treated as a pathological condition. In a homologous way, even if rich Jews in early 1930s Germany "really" *had* exploited German workers, seduced their daughters and dominated the popular press, the Nazis' anti-Semitism would still have been an emphatically "untrue," pathological ideological condition. Why? Because the causes of all social antagonisms were projected onto the "Jew"—an object of perverted love-hatred, a spectral figure of mixed fascination and disgust.

And exactly the same goes for the looting in New Orleans: Even if *all* the reports on violence and rapes had proven to be factually true, the stories circulating about them would still be "pathological" and racist, since what motivated these stories were not facts, but racist prejudices, the satisfaction felt by those who would be able to say: "You see, Blacks really are like that, violent barbarians under the thin layer of civilization!" In other words, we would be dealing with what could be called *lying in the guise of truth:* Even if what I am saying is factually true, the motives that make me say it are false.

ON "NO MAN'S LAND"

After admitting in this essay that I knew nothing at all about gangs, I did a bit of research on the subject. The most useful overview I found was Christopher Adamson's 2000 article "Defensive Localism in White and Black: A Comparative History of European-American and African-American Youth Gangs."

Adamson notes that although white youth gangs have existed since the founding of this nation, black youth gangs did not emerge as a recognized social problem until around 1910. White gangs, now rarer because of suburbanization, were historically widespread, multiethnic, and virulently racist. "Gangs of both races," Adamson writes, "have been predators upon, and protectors of, the communities in which they are embedded. For black and white teenagers, the gang has been a place in which to forge an identity and achieve social status. And just as white youth gangs have attacked vulnerable blacks, black youth gangs have attacked vulnerable whites." For both races, Adamson observes, the gang has helped to defend territory, police neighborhoods, preserve honor, and secure resources.

But while white gangs have served as a route to legitimate power (Richard J. Daley was a member of a gang before becoming mayor of Chicago), black gangs have operated in such isolated and powerless communities that they have not been able to offer their members any opportunities for advancement into the mainstream. Adamson concludes:

> Over the last two hundred years, white youth gangs have facilitated the cultural assimilation of non-Hispanic European immigrants into American society. Irish Catholic, German, Swedish, Polish, Bohemian, Slovak, Lithuanian, Jewish, Italian, Serbian and Greek boys

internalized from the culture of the ethnically mixed gang a sense of whiteness and Americanness. For white immigrants, the youth gang facilitated cultural assimilation because of its close ties with formal and informal political authorities and organizations, which commanded substantial political and economic power. For African Americans, in contrast, the youth gang has reinforced cultural separation because of its embeddedness in racially segregated, economically marginalized and politically powerless communities.

My colleague Bill Savage, a native of Rogers Park, gave me a copy of *Chicago's Far North Side: An Illustrated History of Rogers Park and West Ridge* as a housewarming gift when I moved to the neighborhood. That book, by Neal Samors, Mary Jo Doyle, Martin Lewin, and Michael Williams, served as the source of much of my information about Rogers Park. The *New York Times* article about murder mentioned in this essay is "New York Killers, and Those Killed, by Numbers" by Jo Craven McGinty. Many of my thoughts about gentrification were originally inspired by Molly Hein's wonderful documentary *E. 96th St.*, which explores the border between Harlem and the Upper East Side. And much of my information on Laura Ingalls Wilder came from *Constructing the Little House: Gender, Culture, and Laura Ingalls Wilder* by Ann Romines, and *Laura Ingalls Wilder and the American Frontier*, edited by Dwight Miller.

The page of the 1870 census of Rutland Township, Kansas, on which the name Laura Ingalls is recorded includes a tally at the bottom of the page that lists seven dwellings, fourteen white males, twenty-one white females, three colored males, two colored females, and one foreign-born male and female. Taking into account the fact that five of those whites were second-generation immigrants and that most of the people listed on that page of the census were living in Indian Territory among countless unlisted Indians, one might be inspired to understand Laura Ingalls Wilder's frontier experience as an experience of American diversity.

ON "NOBODY KNOWS YOUR NAME"

The "I See Black People" ads that appeared on billboards and buses in Chicago and other cities in 2006 were part of a marketing campaign for TV One, a cable network specializing in African American programming. These ads played on a line from *The Sixth Sense*—the movie in which a young boy says, "I see dead people." (The parallel between ghosts and blacks suggested by the TV One ads was undone by the addition of a smaller tagline: "living, loving, laughing. . . .") Saladin Patterson's short spoof of *The Sixth Sense*, which quotes lines from the original, features a young boy who says, "I see black people, walking around like they're regular people." His confidant replies, "I don't see anything. Are you sure they're there?"

Names—given, borrowed, and stolen—as Malcolm X reminded us, can haunt our lives. In a 2003 study, researchers at the University of Chicago and MIT found that job applicants with first names common among whites were 50 percent more likely to be offered interviews than identically qualified applicants with first names common among blacks. The researchers sent out five thousand fictional resumes in response to actual want ads in Boston and Chicago, using names gleaned from Massachusetts birth certificates. The names borrowed from white babies included Neil, Brett, Emily, and Anne, and the names borrowed from black babies included Kareem, Tyrone, and Rasheed.

Most of the information about Irish immigrants and laborers in this essay not drawn from Noel Ignatiev's *How the Irish Became White* was drawn from Ronald Takaki's *A Different Mirror: A History of Multicultural America,* which I borrowed from my friend Bill Girard years ago and never returned. (The index of that book includes an evocative series of entries under the heading "Promised Land": "African Americans and," "Chicanos and," "Irish and," "Jews and.")

Matt Wray's *Not Quite White* inspired me to think about white trash as a social group with a distinct history and a unique relationship to race. And some of my thinking about the nature of culture in this essay was informed by John Garvey's essay "My Problem with Multi-Cultural Education," in which he criticizes the multicultural education movement for confusing culture with genetic inheritance and for so often limiting its goals to tolerance. "I would suggest," he writes, "that multi-cultural education is a project of defeat. . . . There was a time when thousands of white households were being rocked by debates between children and parents over the issue of race. But, I would guess, not too much of that goes on now. The abandonment of the struggle over race has been fueled by a conviction that those considered white are not, after all, capable of joining unequivocally in the fight for black liberation and their own freedom."

This essay is for Noel, who named his son John Henry.

ON "ALL APOLOGIES"

Much of the information in this essay was produced by a search for the word "apology" in national newspaper articles from the past thirty years. A number of friends helped me with further research—Kay Beers suggested Janet Holmes's *Women, Men and Politeness,* Yiyun Li explained and translated Chinese apologies, and Ben James gave me a *New York Times* article about Ed Daily's false confession, "The Story Behind a Soldier's Story" by Michael Moss.

Professor of anthropology Allan Young discusses Ed Daily, along with several Vietnam veterans who confessed to atrocities they did not commit, in his 2002 article "The Self-Traumatized Perpetrator as a 'Transient Mental Illness.'" These men, who participated in military action they may have found deeply objectionable even if it was not technically criminal, now imagine themselves criminals who suffer because of their crimes—self-traumatized perpetrators. "In their own eyes," Young explains, "their pain is real and an extension of the victims' suffering." The self-traumatized perpetrator who "becomes a victim as a consequence of being a perpetrator" is a phenomenon, according to Young, mainly limited to the United States. He notes that certain cultural and political conditions encourage the self-traumatized perpetrator to manifest as a disorder, including a society that tends to think of victims and perpetrators as polar opposites. (In such a society, the person who believes himself to be both victim and perpetrator can find psychological release only through a disorder.) And so perhaps our tendency to imagine victims only in opposition to perpetrators is what prevents us from recognizing ourselves as an entire nation of self-traumatized perpetrators—some of us experiencing our trauma as guilt, others as delusion.

When I think about the nature of guilt, I think, inevitably, about "Notes of a Native Son." In that essay James Baldwin writes about the bitterness and anger that destroyed his father, and then about the bitterness and anger he feels toward his father, feelings so closely tied to his feelings about his country that they cannot be untangled. "I saw nothing very clearly," he writes, "but I did see this: that my life, my *real* life, was in danger, and not from anything other people might do but from the hatred I carried in my own heart."

Whenever I read this essay I am moved to wonder if guilt, badly handled, might be just as gangrenous and just as dangerous as hate. If anger is, as Baldwin so often points out, the inevitable inheritance of the black American, then guilt may be the inevitable inheritance of the white American. (This is not a guilt based on individual wrongdoing but on collective responsibility, so if you find the word "guilt" objectionable, think "responsibility" instead. But I prefer "guilt," in part because of its religious associations. We tend to think of guilt as embarrassing and unnecessary now, but it was once imagined, the Old Testament suggests, as an impetus to redemption. The prophet Amos: "Woe to them that are at ease in Zion.") I do believe some atonement is owed, but I think we owe it to ourselves, for the sake of our own salvation.

If America was a young country during slavery, then she is now an adult who must reckon with her childhood. The guilt I have lived with longest and felt most deeply is my guilt over all the debts I will never be able to return to my parents, and over all the impossible apologies I owe them. In this case, I can only hope that my life, which is my crime, might also serve as my apology.

Acknowledgments

Many thanks to the editors of the publications where these essays previously appeared: "Time and Distance Overcome," in the *Iowa Review;* "Relations," in *Identity Theory;* "Three Songs of Salvage," in *P-Queue;* "Land Mines," in *Columbia;* "Goodbye to All That," in the *North American Review;* "Black News," in *Nightsun;* "Letter to Mexico," in *Gulf Coast;* "Babylon," in *Hanging Loose;* "Is This Kansas," in the *Denver Quarterly;* "No Man's Land," in the *Believer;* "Nobody Knows Your Name," in *MAKE;* and "All Apologies," in *Ninth Letter.*

Thanks to Jeff Shotts for his enduring patience and encouragement, and thanks to my agent, Matt McGowan, and all the wonderful folks at Graywolf for the work of publishing this book. Thanks to Robert Polito for reading this book so generously, and thanks to Jeff Clark for his beautiful work on the cover.

Thanks to the Rona Jaffe Foundation, the Vogelstein Foundation, and the Barbara Deming Memorial Fund for financial support while I was working on this book.

Thanks to the friends who discussed these essays with me as I wrote them, across many years and many cities: Mara Naselli, Bonnie Rough, Amy Leach, Halle Shilling, Alex Sheshunoff, Catherine Taylor, and Molly Tambor.

Thanks to the teachers who advised me on this book in its incipient stages: David Hamilton, John D'Agata, and Aimee Carrillo Rowe. And thanks to those good friends who so graciously took on the chore of helping me revise the first full draft of this book: Robyn Schiff, Mary Kinzie, Mavis Biss, and Athan Biss.

Thanks, especially, to John Bresland, for making me think harder and for making everything else easier.

Judge's Afterword

Why must so many essays—to paraphrase Marianne Moore— comport themselves like peacocks, and not, say, humming- birds, owls, or hawks? Despite the nucleus of *assay* in *essay*, contemporary essayists tend to perform their insights, in- stead of inspect, probe, and overturn them. Although I can't remember when I last found a new book of essays so canny, so casually smart, as Eula Biss remarks in "Letter to Mexico" of her stay with a Mexican family in Ensenada, "I did not know, really, anything." Biss's occasions, whether race, iden- tity, geography, space, heredity, or fate, are intractable, even impossible, yet her intricate command and the elegance of her mind in motion originates in doubt, distrust, and self- skepticism. Her voice embraces a devastating mix of insis- tence and quandary, as though she is despairing and pressing on simultaneously—track the restive intelligence inside this passage, for instance, from "Relations," each sentence, nearly every clause, a psychic shift:

If both babies had been white, I might have felt that the white woman was entitled to keep them both, no matter whom they were related to. I might have been wrong, and the courts would very probably not have agreed with me, but I would have believed in her right to keep any child she carried in her womb because that is what I would want for myself. As it was, because one of those babies was black, and because the black woman did not herself conceive—her treatments at the fertility clinic failed and she was childless—it did not seem right for the white woman to keep the black baby. It seemed like a kind of robbery, a robbery made worse by its echoes of history. But even still—and perhaps this exposes how wishful I really am—I wanted to believe in the white woman's desire to maintain a familial connection with the black child. I wanted the two boys to be brothers, and I wanted the original shared-custody agreement to work out. And it might have, especially if the white woman had not made the mistake of saying "come to Mommy" to the black baby on one of those visits, and of calling him by the name she had given him, which was no longer his name.

At the start of "Goodbye to All That," an account of moving to New York, and her honest argument about the city with Joan Didion, Biss slyly glances at the sort of fluent work she resisted writing—"I learned to make my experience of being young and new to the city sound effortless and zany. It was not." For *Notes from No Man's Land* she focuses instead on obstinate contrasts and parallels—those black and white "twins," and various American dolls, including Barbie, Colored Francie, and Biss's own childhood "Black Doll"; her Bronx and Harlem students and the freed slaves during Reconstruction; Babylon and California; looting in New Orleans and Iowa City; her Rogers Park neighborhood and Laura Ingalls Wilder's *Little House on the Prairie.* Operating along the edges of autobiography and history, her "American Essays" are conspicuous for the sweep of American life they insinuate, from "the War on Telephone Poles," Mamie and Kenneth Clark's doll studies, and Don Henley to Buxton, Iowa, the word "nice," and NAFTA. Biss recurrently notes her situation at the periphery of the experiences she scrutinizes—the New York she loved "was the city that existed on the margins of the story," or "I covered a San Diego that did not appear in the travel brochures." Yet her writing from the margins avoids self-congratulation, once more shunning any modish urban strut for personal skepticism. "To imagine oneself as a pioneer in a place as densely populated as Chicago," she writes, "is either to deny the existence of your neighbors or to cast them as natives who must be displaced. Either way, it is a hostile fantasy."

In "Three Songs of Salvage," she quotes an old man fashioning a glass mosaic in his Bed-Stuy garden, "Keep your eyes on the world, okay? . . . Go home and write it all down, every single detail. . . . But don't forget that what you have to capture is the unseen, the imponderable." The recipient of the 2008 Graywolf

Nonfiction Prize, Biss writes essays the way Plutarch and Montaigne did—or if this sounds too classic for her passionate cool, also think James Baldwin, Anne Carson, Jenny Boully, and Luc Sante.

Robert Polito
New Paltz, New York
August 2008

THE GRAYWOLF PRESS NONFICTION PRIZE

Notes from No Man's Land: American Essays by Eula Biss is the 2008 winner of the Graywolf Press Nonfiction Prize. Graywolf awards this prize annually to a previously unpublished, full-length work of outstanding literary nonfiction by a writer who is not yet established in the genre. Previous winners include *Black Glasses Like Clark Kent: A GI's Secret from Postwar Japan* by Terese Svoboda, *Neck Deep and Other Predicaments* by Ander Monson, and *Frantic Transmissions to and from Los Angeles: An Accidental Memoir* by Kate Braverman.

The Graywolf Press Nonfiction Prize seeks to acknowledge—and honor—the great traditions of literary nonfiction, extending from Robert Burton and Thomas Browne in the seventeenth century through Daniel Defoe and Lytton Strachey and on to James Baldwin, Joan Didion, and Jamaica Kincaid in our own time. Whether grounded in observation, autobiography, or research, much of the most beautiful, daring, and original writing over the past few decades can be categorized as nonfiction. Graywolf is excited to increase its commitment to the evolving and dynamic genre.

The prize is judged by Robert Polito, author of *Hollywood & God, Savage Art: A Biography of Jim Thompson, Doubles,* and *A Reader's Guide to James Merrill's "The Changing Light at Sandover,"* and director of the Graduate Writing Program at the New School in New York City.

The Graywolf Press Nonfiction Prize is funded in part by endowed gifts from the Arsham Ohanessian Charitable Remainder Unitrust and the Ruth Easton Fund of the Edelstein Family Foundation.

Arsham Ohanessian, an Armenian born in Iraq who came to the United States in 1952, was an avid reader and a tireless advocate for human rights and peace. He strongly believed in the power of literature and education to make a positive impact on humanity.

 Ruth Easton, born in North Branch, Minnesota, was a Broadway actress in the 1920s and 1930s. The Ruth Easton Fund of the Edelstein Family Foundation is pleased to support the work of emerging artists and writers in her honor.

Graywolf Press is grateful to Arsham Ohanessian and Ruth Easton for their generous support.

EULA BISS is the author of *The Balloonists* and *On Immunity: An Inoculation*. Her essays have appeared in *The Best American Nonrequired Reading* and *The Best Creative Nonfiction*, as well as in the *Believer* and *Harper's*. Her writing has been supported by fellowships from the Guggenheim Foundation, the Howard Foundation, and the National Endowment for the Arts. Biss holds a BA from Hampshire College and an MFA in nonfiction writing from the University of Iowa.

The text of *Notes from No Man's Land* is set in Arno Pro. Book design by Rachel Holscher. Composition by BookMobile Design and Publishing Services, Minneapolis, Minnesota. Manufactured by Versa Press on acid-free 30 percent postconsumer wastepaper.